PARADISE LOST
Books I and II

HARRAP'S ENGLISH CLASSICS

COMUS AND SOME SHORTER POEMS OF MILTON
Edited by E. M. W. TILLYARD, Litt.D., F.B.A., formerly Master of Jesus College, Cambridge
and PHYLLIS B. TILLYARD, M.A., Girton College, Cambridge

MILTON: PARADISE LOST: BOOKS I AND II
Edited by E. M. W. TILLYARD, Litt.D., F.B.A., formerly Master of Jesus College, Cambridge
and PHYLLIS B. TILLYARD, M.A., Girton College, Cambridge

MILTON: PARADISE LOST: BOOKS IX AND X
Edited by E. M. W. TILLYARD, Litt.D., F.B.A., formerly Master of Jesus College, Cambridge

CHAUCER: THE PROLOGUE TO THE CANTERBURY TALES
Edited by R. T. DAVIES, M.A., Lecturer in English Literature, Liverpool University

CHAUCER: THE KNIGHT'S TALE
Edited by J. A. W. BENNETT, M.A., D.Phil., Professor of Mediæval and Renaissance English in the
University of Cambridge

CHAUCER: THE PARDONER'S TALE
Edited by NEVILL COGHILL, M.A., F.R.S.L., formerly Professor of English Literature in the University
of Oxford, *and* CHRISTOPHER TOLKIEN, M.A., Fellow of New College, Oxford

CHAUCER: THE NUN'S PRIEST'S TALE
Edited by NEVILL COGHILL, M.A., F.R.S.L., formerly Professor of English Literature in the University
of Oxford, *and* CHRISTOPHER TOLKIEN, M.A., Fellow of New College, Oxford

TWENTIETH-CENTURY NARRATIVE POEMS
Compiled and edited by MAURICE WOLLMAN, M.A.

TEN TWENTIETH-CENTURY POETS
Edited by MAURICE WOLLMAN, M.A.

A BOOK OF MODERN PROSE
Edited by DOUGLAS BROWN, M.A., formerly of The Perse School, Cambridge

TWENTIETH-CENTURY SHORT STORIES
Edited by DOUGLAS R. BARNES, Senior English Master, Minchenden School, Southgate,
and R. F. EGFORD, Senior English Master, Selhurst Grammar Shcool

NINE TWENTIETH-CENTURY ESSAYISTS
Edited by HAROLD GARDINER, Senior English Master, Bedales School

TEN CONTEMPORARY POETS
Compiled and edited by MAURICE WOLLMAN, M.A.

CHAUCER: THE MAN OF LAW'S TALE
Edited by NEVILL COGHILL, M.A., F.R.S.L., formerly Professor of English Literature in the University
of Oxford, *and* CHRISTOPHER TOLKIEN, M.A., Fellow of New College, Oxford

THE "GREAT CONSULT" OF THE DEVILS

by Doré

High on a throne of royal state which far
Outshone the wealth of Ormus and of Ind . . .

Milton

PARADISE LOST
Books I and II

EDITED WITH AN INTRODUCTION BY

E. M. W. TILLYARD Litt.D., F.B.A.
formerly Master of Jesus College, Cambridge

AND WITH NOTES BY

PHYLLIS B. TILLYARD M.A.
Girton College, Cambridge

GEORGE G. HARRAP & CO. LTD
LONDON TORONTO WELLINGTON SYDNEY

First published in Great Britain 1956
by George G. Harrap & Co. Ltd
182 High Holborn, London, W.C.1

Reprinted: 1960; 1961; 1962; 1963; 1965; 1966; 1969

SBN 245 55882 9

*Composed in Garamond type and printed by
Western Printing Services Ltd, Bristol*

Made in Great Britain

PREFACE

IN preparing the notes of this edition the following books have been found especially useful: Allan H. Gilbert's *A Geographical Dictionary of Milton* and the editions of A. W. Verity, J. C. Scrimgeour, and Merritt Y. Hughes.

E.M.W.T.
P.B.T.

CONTENTS

INTRODUCTION

1. The Initial Difficulties

IT is futile to pretend that *Paradise Lost* as a whole is easy reading; and its first two books are quite as exacting as any of the others. But a great deal of modern poetry is just as difficult; and even poetry that is superficially easy cannot, if it is more than minor verse, be appreciated fully without the cost of some effort. And far more important than the question whether a given poem is easy reading or not is the other question whether it provides a rich return for any trouble expended. It is a question that applies just as surely to Eliot's *Four Quartets* or Pound's *Cantos* as to Milton's *Paradise Lost*. Though, in my experience, few readers today believe that Pound's *Cantos* justify the amount of effort required for the understanding of them, a great many believe that the *Four Quartets* do so; and, having that faith, are willing or even delighted to spend time and effort in their study. Now I do not myself think that the first two books of *Paradise Lost* ultimately repay study better than Books Three and Four or Books Nine and Ten. Indeed, Books Nine and Ten, describing the temptation and the fall of man, their dreadful consequences, and the hope of emerging from them, are more comprehensive and show more sides

of Milton's mind than the first two books. Nevertheless, opinion has favoured these more specialized books
for school use; and the reason is not far to seek. They
contain things which make a quick and sure impression
on the imagination of the general reader: things that
have become as it were proverbial in the wider culture
of Great Britain; the terrible picture of Hell, the figure
of Satan, and the classic debate of the infernal peers.
Here are things, it has been held, that are *obviously* worth
taking trouble over. With them in view it is not unfair
to exact from schoolboys in the highest forms a quite
considerable effort.

It is sometimes said that in understanding *Paradise
Lost* the modern reader is at a disadvantage compared
with the reader of fifty or a hundred years ago. This is
but partly true; and if the modern reader is at a disadvantage in some ways he is better equipped in others.
He knows the Bible and the Classics less well and will
be less at home with Milton's allusions; he is less familiar with the traditional epic form and may be troubled
with Milton's machinery. But he is less open to the
mistake of separating the thought or the theology from
the poetry; and he has learnt, through the complexities
of modern poetry, to respond more quickly than his
predecessor to changes in aim and quality within a
single poem. One of the difficulties of the first two
books of *Paradise Lost* is that when he describes Hell
Milton is sometimes purely descriptive, just building
up his imagined setting, and at other times symbolical,
creating scenes that are hardly visual at all but are the
symbolic renderings of states of mind. A modern
reader will make far less of such a difficulty than would

a reader of fifty years ago. Thus, any idea that it was once fair to expect schoolboys to cope with *Paradise Lost* and that now it is unfair, is false. The difficulties are different but in amount very much the same.

Coming to the difficulties which I have said a modern reader finds in *Paradise Lost*, I will pass over the biblical and classical allusions, for it is the business of the notes to deal with these, and I will confine myself to the traditional epic form. In writing an introduction to some of Milton's short poems I said that the conventions of the modern detective story gave some sort of comparison with the pastoral convention which Milton used in writing *Lycidas*. The best modern comparison I can think of with the inherited form of the epic is the British Coronation Service. That service is antique, in some ways strange, but it possesses an awe and a mystery that render any serious departure from its traditional form unthinkable. It would be easier to destroy it than to change it. *Paradise Lost* is strictly in the tradition of the classical epic; and Milton was strictly in harmony with the temper of his age when he chose to follow that tradition. Spenser, writing his *Faerie Queene* in the age of Elizabeth in deliberate emulation of Virgil's *Aeneid*, was free to depart widely from the form of the classical epic; but during the seventeenth century there arose in Europe the notion that in order to do better than the ancients you had to follow their lead; you had to abide by the rules of the various literary games they had played. This notion grew up in Italy in the century before; and it was thought that Tasso's *Jerusalem Delivered*, which used all the conventions of the classical epic, had got closer to the quality

of Homer and Virgil than any epic of modern times.
Milton wrote *Paradise Lost* in emulation of these three
poets and in so doing he committed himself to following, as it were, a certain ritual. Like parts of the Coronation Service, parts of Milton's ritual in *Paradise Lost*
may appear a little odd to a modern, but he could not
possibly have left them out; to do so would, in the
eyes of his contemporaries, have been a scandal.

Here are two examples, from the first two books of
Paradise Lost, of epic features that Milton felt obliged
to include. The first is the catalogue of the chief devils
in Book One. The action of the poem begins with
Satan's raising himself from the fiery lake and en-
couraging Beelzebub, his second-in-command, to join
him in extricating himself. They spread their wings
and alight on the solid ground that surrounds the lake.
Satan then thinks of his fellows, walks back to the
lake-shore, and calls them. They answer the call, rise
from the lake, and alight where he directs them. Then
he summons the leaders to approach him in order of
rank. The action has been fairly launched; and Milton
now interrupts it with a long and ceremonious account
of the nature and later activities of these leaders, pre-
facing it with a formal invocation of the Muse:

> Say, Muse, their names then known, who first, who last,
> Roused from the slumber on that fiery couch,
> At their great emperor's call, as next in worth
> Came singly where he stood on the bare strand,
> While the promiscuous crowd stood yet aloof.

The authors of the *Iliad* and of the *Aeneid*, the two great
epics of war in antiquity, had included long and ceremonious accounts of the leaders of the armies. Milton

is obliged to do the same, and he introduces his account at just the point of the action where Homer introduced his: that is, at the point where the action has been fairly launched. So ceremonious an account as Milton gives (especially since he assumes in his readers a close familiarity with the Old Testament possessed by few people today) may strike a modern as odd; but by the rules of the game Milton had chosen to play he was bound from the beginning to include it; not to have included it would have been much odder *then* than to include it appears *now*. Actually the account suits Milton's purposes very well. Action in poetry keeps better if punctuated by pauses; and Milton uses his descriptions of the haunts and the characters of the different devils as the means of getting outside Hell and of relating his action to human history, his essential theme. Here, when he followed Homer and Virgil, he was not embarrassed but was able at the same time fully to please himself.

My second example, however, shows Milton a little embarrassed. Having chosen to present a picture of Hell, he was categorically obliged to introduce into it the features of the classical Hades. The most famous of all the books of the *Aeneid* is the sixth; and that describes the descent of Aeneas into the underworld. Essential features of the classical underworld are the five rivers: Lethe, the river of forgetfulness that acts as a boundary and must be crossed by all the souls of the dead in order to enter, and the four doleful streams, Styx, Acheron, Cocytus, and Phlegethon, that are part of the geography of the region which the wicked inhabit. Milton dutifully introduces all five. The four doleful streams give him no difficulty, for they can aptly discharge into his fiery lake and can symbolize the bad passions that possess his devils. Lethe is more difficult. In Plato and in Virgil's *Aeneid* it was used to implement the doctrine of the transmigration of souls. Drinking it a soul forgot his last incarnation and was then ready to be subjected to another when his turn came. But reincarnation is not an orthodox Christian doctrine, and forgetfulness would unduly mitigate the torments of Hell. Lethe has no real business in Milton's picture; yet he is forced to include it. He meets his difficulty by making it a stream of which the devils may never drink, a symbol of the ever-present consciousness of their misery. It is as good a solution as a man could devise; but, left to himself, Milton would probably have been glad to omit the river Lethe altogether. Anyhow, a modern reader should perceive and allow for the conditions under which Milton wrote when he chose the epic form in the middle of the seventeenth century.

In sum, when a modern reader has recognized and faced and accepted and allowed for the two difficulties I have mentioned (the biblical and classical allusions, and the exigencies of the epic form) he is in a perfectly sound position to enjoy the good things that *Paradise Lost* has to give.

2. Milton's Epic Plans

MILTON did not reach the idea of an epic on the fall of man at one stride; and we happen to know something of the processes through which he did reach it. There is evidence that, like Wordsworth and Keats, Milton consciously dedicated himself to poetry at a specific moment of his life. This was at the age of twenty-one; and we need not doubt that from that moment his ambitions included what was then universally considered the highest reach of poetry, the writing of an epic. Further, we know that the kind of epic Milton contemplated was both patriotic and religious. Virgil had celebrated Rome in the *Aeneid*; Milton would celebrate England as his predecessor, Spenser, had done. The great heroic events in English history were, for Milton and most of his English contemporaries, the emergence of England from civil war through the energies of the Tudors, the assertion of religious and national independence through the Reformation, and the defence and establishment of this assertion through the defeat of the Spanish Armada. Milton, again like Virgil, did not intend to use a contemporary setting through which to set forth recent events; but, as Virgil had gone back to the earliest myths about Rome, so Milton proposed to go back to the days of Arthur, with whom the Welsh house of Tudor claimed a mythical connection. In his Latin poem *Mansus*, written at Naples when he was about thirty, he speaks of his poetic plans and of making Arthur and the Round Table, with the defeat of the Saxons, his subject. We can be sure that Arthur would have stood both for a Christian king and for the Tudors, while the heathen Saxons would have stood both for the Turkish infidels that still threatened Europe and the Catholic enemies of English Protestantism. Further, explicit references to recent events would have been introduced through the medium of prophecy, in accordance with the practice of Virgil and Spenser.

The beginnings of the Civil War in 1639 both cut short Milton's European travels and held up his plans for an epic. He had no doubt which side he was on; and in the early days of the war he believed that a Parliamentary victory over the tyrannical Bishops, corrupters of the crown, would bring in a great spiritual betterment throughout the land. And he pictured himself as the poet who should celebrate the victory. It was in these early years of the civil war, when Milton was living in London and conducting a small private school, that he seems to have had a notion of writing a poem on the fall of man. In the library of Trinity College Cambridge there is preserved a manuscript containing the text of most of Milton's shorter poems and jottings concerning future poetic work. These jottings consist of plans for a play or plays; and among many subjects that of Paradise Lost is the most prominent. There is no evidence that Milton meant to substitute a play on the fall of man for the epic on Arthur he had contemplated. On the contrary, he tells us in an autobiographical passage in *Reason of Church Government*, one of his pamphlets against the Bishops, that he is thinking simultaneously of epic, tragedy, and the formal ode as outlets for his high, patriotic, poetical plans.

After 1642, the year when Milton wrote *Reason of Church Government*, and till 1655, when he began on *Paradise Lost*, we have no evidence concerning his plans for poetry. What we can conjecture with certainty is that they depended on the turn of national

events. As long as Milton had faith in his countrymen
and in the leaders of his side in the Civil War he could
contemplate a poem of heroic action, with a hero like
Arthur or Alfred the Great. But when he found that
the victorious Presbyterians were as illiberal and tyrannical as the Episcopalians and when he found his
countrymen feebly going back on their righteous hostility to the house of Stuart, he could no longer put his
heart into the kind of patriotic epic that had been the
rule in the Renaissance. Repudiating nationalism, he
went back to the old medieval theme that antedated the
rise of nationalism in Europe, the theme of Everyman,
of man in general fought for by the powers of good and
evil. That indeed is the innermost theme of *Paradise
Lost*. Though the narrative is based on the beginning
of the *Book of Genesis*, Adam and Eve are hero and
heroine, standing for Everyman and Everywoman, and
God defeats Satan in the battle for their souls.

What, then, we can be certain of is that between
1642 and 1655 Milton altered his conception of the sort
of subject that was apt to his epic and that the subject
he had once intended for a play was now found to
serve for a narrative. It was between these years too
that a great misfortune overtook him, his loss of sight.
But it was a misfortune that had its advantages. On
account of it the exacting post he held under Crom-
well's government became almost a nominal one; and
he at last had leisure to give most of his mind to
poetry, as he had been unable to do since his return
from Italy in 1639. At the age of forty-six he could
settle to the work he had had in mind since the age of
thirty-one.

How Milton composed *Paradise Lost*, in what years
he wrote the different books, we have no means of
judging. All we know is that he probably began
serious work of it in 1655 and that it was first printed
in 1667.

3. The Theme of "Paradise Lost"

THE first two books of *Paradise Lost* form a complete
section within the whole poem; but in spite of this
completeness they cannot be fully understood out of
their context. In this section I try to explain, for the
benefit of those who have not read the whole poem,
what this context is.

I have said that when Milton abandoned his idea of
a martial, patriotic epic he turned to the medieval subject of Everyman and displayed Adam and Eve fought
over by the powers of good and evil. This is true as far
as it goes, but in depicting the fight Milton also gave
his version of the essential scheme of Christian theology and of the course of world history; he made his
subject as wide-embracing as it is possible to imagine.
Among his epic predecessors only Dante had included
so much. Further, Milton was vividly aware that the
present moment, life as actually lived now, was part of
the eternal process. Adam and Eve are not only figures
in the Old Testament and types of humanity at large;
they are types also of ourselves now. Nowhere is this
more evident than at the end of the poem, which describes Adam and Eve expelled by God's angels from

Paradise and left to make the best of life outside it. These are the last five lines:

> Some natural tears they dropped, but wiped them soon;
> The world was all before them, where to choose
> Their place of rest, and Providence their guide:
> They hand in hand with wand'ring steps and slow,
> Through Eden took their solitary way.

Adam and Eve are no longer archetypal, heroic figures. They are ordinary man and woman, faced with the ordinary problems of life in this world, granted wide choice of good and evil on their own initiative, prone to err and yet free to correct error by reliance on God.

I stress Milton's constant awareness of actual life as it is now lived because in apparent subject-matter the first two books are the remotest possible from the life of every day. There is no human character, and the setting is deliberately alien to that of normal humanity on earth. You might think it was simply not worth looking for the life of every day in Milton's Hell and Chaos. Yet even a casual inspection shows how well Milton succeeds in humanizing his opening books. Though his devils are figures with superhuman proportions, their minds work like human minds, and their deliberations are on the pattern of human politics. Further, in his comparisons Milton constantly lets human history and ordinary life into the context of Hell. His devils turn out to be the heathen gods of the Old Testament and of classical mythology, and as such they point to whole areas of history. In the similes we have our attention turned to homely things that were quite accepted and commonplace in Milton's day: to benighted fishermen, to the pipes of an organ, to a peasant with his superstitious belief in fairies, to arguments on predestination and free will. Just as the *Aeneid* was about the Rome of Augustus as well as about the great workings of fate that created Rome in the beginning and built up its greatness, so is *Paradise Lost* about life as lived now in Milton's time as well as about the great scheme under which all life was created and is transacted. And where Milton triumphs is in making the two themes inseparable: for him life today is also life in eternity.

4. The Scheme of "Paradise Lost"

THERE is little story involved in what I have called the theme of *Paradise Lost*. But Milton chose to express his theme not by direct exposition, as in a sermon, but through a verse narrative; and this choice meant a story.

Being virtually compelled through the public opinion of the age in which he lived to tell his story in the manner of the classical writers of epic, he must concentrate his action into a small span and include things outside that span through the methods of retrospective narrative and of prophecy. His theme was mankind in its complete historical setting fought over by the powers of good and evil. In this fight there were several stages. Taking the creation of the angels for granted and any ages of their undivided loyalty to God we care to imagine, we can say that, in the theological scheme Milton inherited and used, the first event in the fight was Satan's revolt in Heaven, which detached a portion of the angels to his side. After that revolt there was war in Heaven, at the end of which Satan and his crew were thrown out and fell through Chaos into the Hell which God had made out of part of Chaos to receive them. Meanwhile, God created the universe and its occupants, vegetable, animal, and human, as narrated at the beginning of the Bible. He gives the two first human beings, Adam and Eve, a garden to live in and with it the freedom of everything except the fruit of a single tree. In forbidding them to eat this fruit he tests their souls with a view to saving them. But he allows Satan to try to seduce them, and Satan succeeds. Thus Adam and Eve and their descendants are corrupted. Not completely, however, for the earth still contains a few virtuous men. But mankind cannot shed its corruption by its own efforts; hence, so far, Satan has had the best of the fight. God retaliates by submitting his son to the abasement of human incarnation. Having become man Christ can act as man's proxy and deal with Satan. He defeats Satan first by resisting his temptations in the wilderness and second by redeeming, through the gift of his own life on the cross, the loss of life Adam incurred through disobeying God's command in the garden. Mankind is now free to obtain salvation and everlasting life if it chooses to profit by Christ's sacrifice.

In this scheme of cosmic history there are four decisive acts: the revolt of Satan, the disobedience of man, Christ's resistance to Satan's temptations in the wilderness, and Christ's redeeming death. To any one wishing to recount the whole of world history as related to the scheme the first of these decisive acts would be inconvenient as coming too early in the series and as leaving so much of the total happenings in the future, not to be dealt with except through prophecy. Milton chose the second act for his principal poem and the third for his shorter narrative poem, *Paradise Regained*. Before his day there had been narrative poems on the crucifixion; the noblest rendering of it in English being certain parts of Langland's *Piers Plowman*. Langland put his greatest stress on the immediate consequence of the crucifixion as recorded in medieval legend, the so-called Harrowing (*i.e.*, subduing) of Hell. The legend was an expansion of the sentence in the Apostles' Creed, "he descended into Hell"; and it recounted Christ's breaking through the gates of Hell and releasing Adam and Eve from the prison, where they had been captive for 4000 years. Christ's act brought full circle the process that began with the original temptation in Paradise. By Milton's day the legend of the Harrowing of Hell, which had meant so much to the Middle Ages and which lent itself so well to dramatic treatment, had lost favour with Catholics and Protestants alike. It was not really available for him.

Milton, then, chose the disobedience and fall of man as the central acts round which to group, first, the drama of good and evil fighting for Everyman and, second, the course of world-history. But you cannot understand what he was doing unless you see that in these central acts he included the repentance and the virtual salvation of Adam and Eve, anticipating the redemptive process which, strictly speaking, did not take place till the Incarnation. By taking this liberty Milton was able vastly to extend the scope of his poem. Aristotle in his *Poetics* said that the best kind of tragic plot contains what he calls *peripeteia*, a word which a recent translator has rendered by *irony*. There is *peripeteia* when events which seem to tend in one direction actually take another. Milton must have followed the orthodox scholarly opinion of his day in thinking that most of the things that were advisable in tragedy were advisable in the epic also. Now, by enlarging the scope of the acts round which everything else is grouped Milton was able to contrive a great irony, which dominates his central episodes and has its effect on the rest of the poems, the two first books included. The irony is that the action that seems to lead to destruction, the disobedience of Adam and Eve, and which does indeed cause terrible havoc and suffering, unexpectedly has a happy issue in their repentance and in their forgiveness by God. And the irony is at the expense of Satan. He had revolted from God and he concluded that if he could persuade Adam and Eve to revolt, they, like him, must be quite perverted to evil. He forgot that his own crime was worse than theirs: it was entirely of his own choosing; while theirs was partly the fault of himself, who deceived them. Satan then is thwarted in his fight through this *peripeteia*: what appeared to him inevitably to lead one way actually led another. The forces of good have won, and the souls of Adam and Eve have been saved, as may be saved the souls of any mortals who genuinely seek the salvation offered. In this way *Paradise Lost* is not, as often thought, an utterly tragic book with a pessimistic view of life. Good does thwart evil. And yet the price Adam and his

descendants have had to pay for their crimes is great.
Sin and death have indeed entered the world; and Paradise is no longer the crown of a happy existence but
the reward of humble endurance. Milton is acutely
aware of the inextricable interlocking of good and ill
in life as actually experienced.

5. The Construction of "Paradise Lost"

MILTON could have treated his theme in different ways;
and I go on to describe the way he disposed it. From
this description it should be plain how the first two
books serve the general plan.

Writing in the mode of the classical epic, Milton
begins his story in the middle of the total action. The
bad angels have already revolted and been defeated,
and God has already created Hell and the universe,
when Satan recovers consciousness and raises his head
from the fiery lake in which he is lying helpless. After
he has roused himself and his fellows and inspired them
with new courage, further action is made to hinge on
the rumour current in Heaven before the angels fell
that God was about to create a new kind of being. The
devils decide that the best way to carry on the war
against God is to seek to corrupt this new creation.
Satan is entrusted with the mission and meets his offspring, Sin and Death, at Hell's gate. They band themselves into a Trinity, which corresponds to and parodies
the Trinity of Heaven. Satan travels through Chaos to
the borders of light and sees the towers of Heaven and

the universe hanging from it by a chain. This ends the
first two books. But not only do these books promote
the plot; they also constitute a single motive, or in
musical phrase a movement. The motive is that of Hell
or of the complex of evil forces that is seeking to ruin
Everyman or Adam and Eve.

The third book opens with a long invocation of
light, symbol of the divine and the good, which marks
the statement of the second motive, Heaven. The felicity
of Heaven is described so as to match the miseries of
Hell; and, as Satan offered to go out alone to corrupt
mankind, so the Son offers to undergo a lonely incarnation in order to save it. Having described Heaven,
Milton continues the journey of Satan till he penetrates
the globe of the universe that contains the stars and
the planets and Earth in the centre, and lands on the
Earth.

It is now time for the human protagonists to be introduced; and in the fourth book Milton describes the
garden of Paradise and its human and animal inhabitants, letting us know as he does this that Adam and
Eve are prohibited the use of a single tree in the garden.
Meanwhile Satan, disguised, enters the garden and,
when Eve is asleep, insinuates an evil dream into her
ear. The guardian-angels set to watch discover him and
drive him out. So ends his first attempt to corrupt Eve.

Satan having been foiled, there is a pause in the
action, and Milton uses it for narrating past events.
The fifth and sixth books contain the visit of the Arch-
angel Raphael to Paradise and the account he gives
Adam and Eve of the revolt and fall of the angels.
Though Raphael's visit extends for two more books,

Milton in his prologue to the seventh tells us that now his stage is purely earthly; he has done with his vaster setting; the rest of the poem centres on man. So now Adam sets the pace and wants to know how the universe in which he dwells came into being. Raphael recounts the six days of creation. In the eighth book Adam asks more questions about the universe and then recounts what happened to him since his first dawn of consciousness. After which Raphael, having earnestly warned Adam not to transgress God's prohibition, returns to Heaven.

The main action is resumed in the ninth book and reaches its crisis in it and in the tenth. With the crisis comes a change of tone, to which Milton points in his prologue to Book Nine. There he says that he is changing his former style to tragic; and we do indeed now feel ourselves right in the centre of real human experience. Satan, disguised as a serpent, renews his attack. He has the luck to find Eve alone and by lies and flattery persuades her to eat the forbidden fruit. Adam, finding her, eats also, and they are both incriminated. The fruit first intoxicates and then leaves them disillusioned. The ninth book ends with a quarrel and mutual recrimination. Satan to all appearances has triumphed. But the main action has been but half transacted. The Son goes to Paradise to pass sentence on Adam and Eve for their sin. He condemns them to hardships on earth followed by death; but he also pities and clothes them. Then the effects of man's fall show themselves. The climate changes, the animals make war on one another, Sin and Death build a causeway through Chaos giving easy transit between Hell's mouth and the entrance to the universe. Adam falls into despair on seeing these happenings and thinks himself lost for ever. Then Eve decides that to be at variance with Adam is intolerable and wishes to take all the blame on herself. Adam at first rebuffs her but in the end, helped unwittingly by God's grace and not in himself totally corrupted by his disobedience, admits his own fault too, and they are reconciled. This act of common humility is the salvation of Adam and Eve; and the tenth book ends with their asking God's pardon

> with tears
> Watering the ground, and with their sighs the air
> Frequenting, sent from hearts contrite, in sign
> Of sorrow unfeigned and humiliation meek.

Once Adam and Eve repent, the issue is certain, and the last two books deal almost entirely with future events. God, having accepted the pair's contrition, sends Michael, the great warrior archangel, to grant them a prophetic vision of the world's history. They see a series of tableaux of the main events described in *Genesis* up to the Flood; the point at which the eleventh book ends. Then in the twelfth and last book Michael summarizes history in his own words from the Flood till the day of doom, the happenings recounted in the New Testament included. Adam realizes now the nature of things and he accepts it; he has learnt obedience; he knows that Christian humility is stronger in the end than Satanic pride. And Adam and Eve are fortified with this knowledge when Michael leaves them and his guard of angels expel them from Paradise to seek their fortune in the wider world.

6. Milton's Cosmos

THOUGH Milton was skilled in vast suggestive pictures, he was quite clear on the configuration of his universe. I do not mean that Milton believed these things literally. He lived in the pre-scientific age when the limits of belief were far less sharply defined than they came to be in the nineteenth century. People then did not always trouble to distinguish between actual happenings and acceptable metaphor. Certainly Milton did not believe literally in the geography of his Hell or in the physical

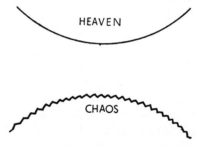

embodiment of Sin. What I mean is that within the poem the imagined landscape is precise and needs to be realized for the proper appreciation of the poem.

One cannot describe Milton's cosmos simply because it was in process of growth during the course of the poem. We have to imagine a time when the sum of created things consisted of Heaven or the empyrean, bounded by a crystal wall, and, at an indeterminate distance below it, the dark mass of Chaos, the confused and jarring material of possible future creation. Between the two was an open region enjoying heaven's light, and, as Satan found in his journey described at the end of the second book, there was a frontier, where chaos thinned out and neither darkness nor light but twilight prevailed. The simple diagram given on the previous page will illustrate.

When the bad angels were expelled from Heaven, God created a prison, Hell, to receive them. It was situated at the very bottom of Chaos and it was vaulted over and closed at the top of the vault with gates. The diagram then has to be changed as follows:

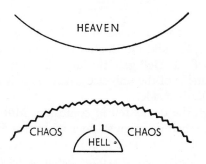

The final act of creation was for God to take more of the material of Chaos and to create the universe. There is no need to describe here the internal mechanism of the universe with the earth in the middle and the concentric spheres with the planets and fixed stars around, for it does not concern the books of *Paradise Lost* in question. But the reader needs to know that the universe was enclosed by a solid shell, that there was an opening at the top of this shell, through which the angels and later the devils could pass in order to visit mankind, and that a golden chain connected the universe with Heaven. We thus get this third diagram:

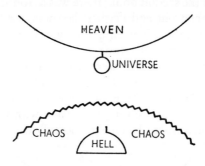

Last of all, as we are told in Book Two it is destined to happen, Sin and Death after the fall of man build a causeway from Hell-gate through Chaos to the point on the outside of the universe where there is the opening that leads inside.

Though the devils fell in confusion, Milton makes them keep their different stations when they have risen from the fiery lake. This is most evident when he pictures the leaders approaching Satan as he stands by the lake-side, singly, in order of seniority. Milton does this because he still retains traces of the medieval idea of a world organized with a kind of mathematical regularity. The feudal organization of society was both elaborate and accurately graded. And if human society was thus graded, so had heavenly society to be. In the most generally accepted account the angels were arranged in a fixed order according to their natural capacity to receive the divine essence. Those of inferior capacity received it through the medium of their superiors. There were three main classes of angels and each class had three divisions. The highest class was contemplative and consisted of Seraphs, Cherubs, and Thrones. The next class was partly contemplative and partly active and consisted of Dominations, Virtues, and Powers. More active still was the third class, and it consisted of Principalities, Archangels, and Angels. It is this lowest division, the Angels, who go on God's errands. Corresponding to the nine divisions of Angels were nine of Devils. Milton made use of some of this medieval lore, but by his day the old medieval precision had been abandoned. Although he was in the medieval tradition in making Satan, Beelzebub, and Mammon important individual devils, he abandoned the medieval classes of devils and uses the angelic classes for fallen as well as unfallen Angels. Also in using those classes he alters the order of their dignity. He makes the Archangels the highest division, higher than the Seraphs and Cherubs. Nor does he distinguish the relative importance of Thrones, or Virtues, or Powers; and he can make the word "Powers" cover all classes of Angel. He was in fact more interested in the idea of there being an order than in the precise nature of it. Hence his frequent use of the words *hierarch* and *hierarchy*. When he uses those words he wants us to think of the principle of orderly arrangement throughout the cosmos.

Not only did medieval people like to think of all creation arranged in a sequence, they liked also to find correspondences everywhere. I have just mentioned the nine orders of devils corresponding to the nine orders of angels. They thought it fitting that as the Devil corrupted man in the garden of Paradise and caused him to exchange Paradise for a wilderness, so Christ, the second Adam, defeated the Devil's temptations in the wilderness and restored Paradise to the first Adam. Milton's invention of the trinity of Satan, Sin, and Death to correspond to the Christian Trinity illustrates the same habit of mind. It is a valuable habit, for it makes for tightness of poetic structure.

So much for the nature of *Paradise Lost* in general. I pass to some special points in Books One and Two.

7. Description in Books I and II

MORE than one writer has pronounced with confidence that Milton's descriptions are grand but imprecise; and the pronouncement can be intended as either praise or blame. And it is true that when at the end of Book Two Satan emerges from Chaos and sees "far off the empyreal Heaven," it is described vaguely as

> extended wide
> In circuit, undetermined square or round.

Yet this vagueness is set in a very precise description of Chaos thinning out into an "emptier waste resembling air" and of Satan's thence seeing the universe hanging from the heavenly region by a golden chain. I fancy that Milton deliberately kept Heaven vague because he meant to suggest that Satan could not bear to view it closely, while he made a clear picture of the borders of Chaos and of the pendent world bathed in the light of Heaven because it is there that Satan's energies are to be directed. My main point, however, is that you cannot generalize about Milton's descriptions, which can be precise, vague, or purely symbolical, as he thinks the context requires. I will give examples of his different methods.

I have already mentioned the precise details of Satan's movements from his rising out of the fiery lake to his reviewing of the mustered devils. Satan stands by the lake-side (and it is legitimate, though not necessary, to imagine that he selected a spot where the ground rose and that Beelzebub stood near him as second-in-command), and one by one the highest officers detach themselves from the body of devils, mustered at some distance from Satan, and cross the intervening plain. Milton's account makes a picture, or rather provides us with the means of enabling each reader to make his own clear picture. On the other hand Milton is careful not to be too precise about Hell, knowing that it is more dreadful if kept vague. It is a prison, and we know it is vaulted; but we are not made to picture any rigidly bounding roof: on the contrary our impression is of indeterminate expanse and the horror of doubtful gloom. The fiery lake from which Satan arises and the burning land on which he alights are described *approximately*. *Lake* and *land* are mere shots at description, not accurate renderings:

> if it were land, that ever burned
> With solid, as the lake with liquid fire.

And Milton can describe the atmosphere of Hell only by contradictions. There is "utter darkness" in Hell, and yet Hell's flames provide "a darkness visible." In the account of the building of Pandemonium there is, again, a mixture of the precise and the vague. Milton tells us exactly how the metal was prepared and he may even mean us to admire the ingenuity of the devils in putting the fiery lake to a practical, industrial use. But he does not tell us how the devil-workers shaped the rising mass of malleable ore into the building

> where pilasters round
> Were set, and Doric pillars overlaid
> With golden architrave.

And he had his reasons. He humanizes his devils when he gives them precise occupations, thus making them interesting; and he makes them also masters of a super-human magic when he omits any precise reference to the way the building is shaped.

Throughout Book One the descriptions, precise or vague, are genuine descriptions serving to create in our minds imagined pictures. But in Book Two, after the council has been dissolved and the cherubim have announced its conclusions, description takes a very different turn. Its subject is the various amusements of the devils while Satan is absent on his great mission. Some indulge in terrestrial or aerial horse-racing; others prefer grosser sports and throw rocks and hills about. The intellectuals retire to a quiet valley and amuse themselves with poetry and with talking philosophy. All these things are put in a setting so different from the former that they should at once declare themselves as imagined under a different set of premises. The silent

valley especially is hopelessly at odds with the established geography of Hell. Milton has in fact passed
from visual to symbolic description. He does not mean
us to add the horse-racing and the quiet valley to the
existing account of Hell; he means us to see them as
restricted symbols of the devils' state of mind. Thus
taken, they form a marvellous summary of the different ways people seek to escape from a wretched
actuality, whether of active misery or of mere boredom:
sport, controlled or unruly, music, poetry, philosophy.
And later when another section of the devils go exploring, he adds travel to the list. Not that Milton condemned or undervalued these things (except the unruly
sports); on the contrary he prized them greatly. But he
knew how hollow they all are without a wholesome
and settled state of soul. The picture of the devils,
their own minds enslaved by unruly and tormenting
passions, weaving their abstract philosophical theories,
is one of an almost tragic irony. It is into this series of
symbolic descriptions that Milton inserts those references to the classical Hades it would be improper for
him to omit. Coming here and not in the more truly
descriptive accounts of Hell they are much more appropriate.

There is another reason why Milton changed the
nature of his descriptions. He was about to bring Satan
face to face with the extraordinary allegorical figures
of Sin and Death. The descriptions of the figures are
monstrous and violent; and to give them immediately
after the political realism of the devils' debate would
have been disastrous. A transition was necessary; and
Milton provides it by his symbolic landscape and the

occupations of the devils that symbolize states of mind. There is no doubt about the power with which Milton describes Sin and Death and the threatened conflict between them and Satan. But there is one detail to which I cannot reconcile myself. We cannot forget that Milton has partly humanized Satan; it is because he is human that Satan can stir our feelings so strongly. But there is something inappropriate in so human a figure giving birth to the allegorical figure of an abstraction. The process should be the other way round. Out of the abstraction, to which no limits need be set, should come the vast yet more limited and in some ways human figure of the prince of Hell.

8. Satan

IF some critics have written too simply about Milton's methods of description, so have they about Satan. Some have made him the poem's hero, others have tried to reduce him to a ludicrous and contemptible figure. The truth is that he is a complex character, an archangel ruined, as Milton says he is. He retains the stature and some of the nobility of an archangel, but he is also degraded. And it is precisely this combination that makes him so interesting and so tragic. "Corruption of the best is ever the worst corruption" was a truth that Milton was well aware of; and the old notion that Satan ran away with his creator and ended by being better than had first been meant is superfluous. Milton knew exactly what he was doing.

Those who have written Satan up as a hero have forgotten how self-deceived he is from the beginning, how stupid in refusing to accept the truth. After Beelzebub in his first speech has stated the sad truth that God is indeed almighty, Satan persists in thinking that he can distort God's designs:

> If then his providence
> Out of our evil seek to bring forth good,
> Our labour must be to pervert that end,
> And out of good still to find means of evil,
> Which oft times may succeed.

Satan is a stronger character and has a better intelligence than Beelzebub; yet he is so corrupted by pride that here he is stupid where Beelzebub shows sense. Milton makes Satan's stupidity particularly clear at the beginning of Book Two. He is "by success [*i.e.*, the issue of events] untaught"; he has become too stupid to learn by experience. The tragedy of Satan reaches its height when he reviews his embattled devils:

> He through the armed files
> Darts his experienced eye, and soon traverse
> The whole battalion views, their order due,
> Their visages and stature as of gods;
> Their number last he sums. And now his heart
> Distends with pride, and hardening in his strength
> Glories.

What is so terrible here is Satan's vulgarity in making so much of mere size and numbers. His sentiment is quite unworthy of his other sentiments in the famous passage that comes soon after, when his courage and resolution and pride are crossed by remorse and he weeps three times before he can speak. It is by putting these two passages together that we can see the capaciousness of Satan's character and its contradictions. When we find Satan stupid and vulgar we must remember that in his natural endowment he had a brilliant mind and the highest magnanimity. And when we find him magnificent in resolution and displaying the remnants of his natural magnanimity we must remember that those splendid qualities are rendered tragically futile by his corruption.

People will go on discussing Satan's character as they will go on discussing the motives of Hamlet. And the reason is its extraordinary suggestiveness. He is the classic rendering of greatness corrupted, something of eternal recurrence in the world, of which every adult has had some knowledge. And it is natural to refer what knowledge we have to Milton's Satan, whose function is to sum it up and to complete it in a way we cannot do ourselves.

9. The Devils' Council

I HAVE said that Milton keeps on introducing human concerns into his Hell, mindful that his chief object was to give a picture of human fate as valid for the year in which he was writing as for any other year in human history. And in the main he works through the human references in his similes. But in one episode, the council in Book Two, he comes near to making Hell itself human. It is likely, though not at all certain, that Milton wrote the first two books of *Paradise Lost* before the

Restoration, while he was still Latin Secretary. The duties of the post were to draft despatches to foreign powers in what was then the language of diplomacy, Latin. We should now call him a civil servant working for the Foreign Office. His post brought him into close contact with politicians; and there can be no doubt that the devils' debate owes part of the conviction it carries to Milton's political contacts.

It is true that all the sharers in the debate are bad; and yet they stand for perpetual political types. Moloch is the type of person who reduces everything to a sharp simple issue and puts all his strength behind it. In Milton's context he is desperate in his despair and futile; but men of his type of mind, if they are also of good will, can become leaders at a time of crisis when issues are simple and single-hearted courage is the only relevant mood. Belial is Moloch's perfect foil. He has a superb façade and a subtler understanding than Moloch. But he is lazy, and his will is corrupt. And this laziness fools him into imagining that God will relax his vigilance if unprovoked. He is indeed the eternal type of the political appeaser, the man who refuses to face the present truth, who tries to make do with things as they are in the hope that something unexpected will turn up; as Belial says,

> Besides what hope the never-ending flight
> Of future days may bring, what chance, what change
> Worth waiting.

Appeasers need not be bad men in themselves; they may have the best of wills; and thus Belial stands not only for the ill-willed temporizers but for them all. Mammon is more active than Belial and more of a realist. He knows that submission and "forced hallelujahs" are out of the question but he refuses to abandon all hope of action. Beelzebub is the accomplished politician. Where the others had gone straight to the point, he opens his speech formally and flatters his audience. He has the great advantage of having up his sleeve a plan that suits the true desires of the audience. He knows the 'sense of the meeting' beforehand and he times his proposal just right. Further, he and Satan (as a chairman and a secretary always should do) had discussed the agenda beforehand:

> Thus Beelzebub
> Pleaded his devilish counsel, first devised
> By Satan and in part proposed.

And when Satan offers to make the perilous journey to earth alone, we can be certain that he and Beelzebub had carefully staged the dramatic setting of the offer beforehand.

Milton's great political sagacity reassures us that in spite of the monstrousness of Hell itself and of the figures of Sin and Death he never loses sight of the great general truths of human nature.

10. Prosody and Style

It is strange that school editions of *Paradise Lost* usually contain a section on the prosody whereas school editions of Shakespeare's plays usually do not: as if Shakespeare wrote blank verse by nature and Milton on a preconceived metrical scheme. Nothing could be more mistaken. They both inherited a common metre and used it in the ways that best suited their purposes. It is convenient to know some system of prosody in order to be able to describe different kinds of blank verse or other kinds of metre; but that convenience applies equally to all verse. And more important than a knowledge of a prosodical system is the ability to *read* a given piece of blank verse: to get the emphasis and the pauses and the weight of syllables right. These are things which, if treated in an edition, would swell an introduction to an inordinate length; and they should be the concern of the teacher in co-operation with any pupils who have a gift for such matters.

As for Milton's style, I repeat the warnings I gave when writing of his descriptions and of the character of Satan. Beware of making it out simpler than it is. Writers have called it sublime or latinized or elaborate or what not, and up to a point they have been right. But Milton never confined himself to any set way of writing. Take his account of Moloch in Book Two:

> His trust was with the Eternal to be deemed
> Equal in strength, and rather than be less
> Cared not to be atall; with that care lost
> Went all his fear: of God, or Hell, or worse
> He recked not.

Here Milton is emphatic enough but how unadorned and unlatinized and uninflated! None of the usual adjectives descriptive of his style fit the passage. And this one example can serve to demonstrate the truth that Milton is far too great and varied a poet to be bound by easy generalizations. The right course is to take him without rigid predispositions, to be open to what he offers you, to enjoy him for what he is and not for

what you have been told, or have imagined beforehand, he ought to be.

11. The Text

Paradise Lost was first published in 1667, in ten books;
and there were new impressions of this first edition in
the next two years. In 1674 Milton published a revised
edition, introducing a few changes into the text and
dividing the original Books Seven and Ten into two so
as to make twelve books in all after the manner of
Virgil. The text here given is nearly always that of
1674, with spelling modernized and some changes in
the punctuation.

12. Bibliography

The following books may be found useful for further reading:

Bush, Douglas, *Paradise Lost in our Time* (Oxford University Press, 1945).

Grierson, H. J. C., *Milton and Wordsworth* (Cambridge
University Press, 1937).

✓ Lewis, C. S., *A Preface to Paradise Lost* (Oxford University Press, 1942).

Muir, Kenneth, *John Milton* (Longmans, Green, 1955).

Raleigh, Walter, *Milton* (Edward Arnold, 1900).

✓ Tillyard, E. M. W., *Milton* (Chatto and Windus, 1930);
Studies in Milton (Chatto and Windus, 1951).

Warner, Rex, *John Milton* (Max Parrish, 1950).

Waldock, A. J. A., *Paradise Lost and its Critics* (Cambridge University Press, 1947).

PARADISE LOST

Book I

Of Man's first disobedience, and the fruit
Of that forbidden tree, whose mortal taste
Brought death into the world, and all our woe,
With loss of Eden, till one greater Man
Restore us, and regain the blissful seat,   5
Sing, heavenly Muse, that on the secret top
Of Oreb, or of Sinai, didst inspire
That shepherd, who first taught the chosen seed
In the beginning how the Heavens and Earth
Rose out of Chaos: or, if Sion hill   10
Delight thee more, and Siloa's brook that flowed
Fast by the oracle of God, I thence
Invoke thy aid to my adventurous song,
That with no middle flight intends to soar
Above the Aonian mount, while it pursues   15
Things unattempted yet in prose or rhyme.
And chiefly thou, O Spirit, that dost prefer
Before all temples the upright heart and pure,
Instruct me, for thou know'st; thou from the first
Wast present, and with mighty wings outspread   20
Dove-like sat'st brooding on the vast Abyss
And mad'st it pregnant: what in me is dark
Illumine, what is low raise and support;

That to the highth of this great argument
I may assert eternal Providence,   25
And justify the ways of God to men.

    Say first (for Heaven hides nothing from thy view,
Nor the deep tract of Hell) say first what cause
Moved our grand parents, in that happy state,
Favoured of Heaven so highly, to fall off   30
From their Creator, and transgress his will
For one restraint, lords of the world besides.
Who first seduced them to that foul revolt?
The infernal serpent; he it was, whose guile,
Stirred up with envy and revenge, deceived   35
The mother of mankind, what time his pride
Had cast him out from Heaven, with all his host
Of rebel angels, by whose aid, aspiring
To set himself in glory above his peers,
He trusted to have equalled the Most High,   40
If he opposed; and with ambitious aim
Against the throne and monarchy of God
Raised impious war in Heaven and battle proud
With vain attempt. Him the Almighty Power
Hurled headlong flaming from the ethereal sky   45
With hideous ruin and combustion down
To bottomless perdition; there to dwell
In adamantine chains and penal fire,
Who durst defy the Omnipotent to arms.

    Nine times the space that measures day and night 50
To mortal men, he with his horrid crew
Lay vanquished, rolling in the fiery gulf,
Confounded though immortal. But his doom
Reserved him to more wrath; for now the thought
Both of lost happiness and lasting pain   55

Torments him: round he throws his baleful eyes,
That witnessed huge affliction and dismay,
Mixed with obdurate pride and steadfast hate.
At once, as far as angels ken, he views
The dismal situation waste and wild: 60
A dungeon horrible, on all sides round,
As one great furnace flamed; yet from those flames
No light, but rather darkness visible
Served only to discover sights of woe,
Regions of sorrow, doleful shades, where peace   65
And rest can never dwell, hope never comes
That comes to all; but torture without end
Still urges, and a fiery deluge, fed
With ever-burning sulphur unconsumed.
Such place eternal justice had prepared   70
For those rebellious; here their prison ordained
In utter darkness, and their portion set
As far removed from God and light of Heaven
As from the centre thrice to the utmost pole.
Oh how unlike the place from whence they fell!   75
There the companions of his fall, o'erwhelmed
With floods and whirlwinds of tempestuous fire,
He soon discerns; and weltering by his side
One next himself in power and next in crime,
Long after known in Palestine and named   80
Beëlzebub. To whom the arch-enemy,
And thence in Heaven called Satan, with bold words
Breaking the horrid silence, thus began:
    "If thou beest he—but Oh how fallen! how changed
From him, who in the happy realms of light,   85
Clothed with transcendent brightness, didst outshine
Myriads, though bright! if he whom mutual league,

United thoughts and counsels, equal hope
And hazard in the glorious enterprise,
Joined with me once, now misery hath joined 90
In equal ruin: into what pit thou seest
From what highth fallen, so much the stronger proved
He with his thunder: and till then who knew
The force of those dire arms? yet not for those,
Nor what the potent victor in his rage 95
Can else inflict, do I repent, or change,
Though changed in outward lustre, that fixed mind,
And high disdain from sense of injured merit,
That with the Mightiest raised me to contend,
And to the fierce contention brought along 100
Innumerable force of spirits armed,
That durst dislike his reign, and, me preferring,
His utmost power with adverse power opposed
In dubious battle on the plains of Heaven,
And shook his throne. What though the field be
    lost? 105
All is not lost: the unconquerable will,
And study of revenge, immortal hate,
And courage never to submit or yield;
And what is else not to be overcome?
That glory never shall his wrath or might 110
Extort from me. To bow and sue for grace
With suppliant knee, and deify his power
Who, from the terror of this arm, so late
Doubted his empire: that were low indeed;
That were an ignominy and shame beneath 115
This downfall; since by fate the strength of gods
And this empyreal substance cannot fail;
Since, through experience of this great event,

In arms not worse, in foresight much advanced,
We may with more successful hope resolve   120
To wage by force or guile eternal war,
Irreconcilable to our grand foe,
Who now triumphs, and in the excess of joy
Sole reigning holds the tyranny of Heaven."
    So spake the apostate angel, though in pain,   125
Vaunting aloud, but racked with deep despair;
And him thus answered soon his bold compeer:
    "O Prince, O chief of many thronèd powers,
That led the embattled Seraphim to war
Under thy conduct, and, in dreadful deeds   130
Fearless, endangered Heaven's perpetual king,
And put to proof his high supremacy,
Whether upheld by strength, or chance, or fate,
Too well I see and rue the dire event
That with sad overthrow and foul defeat   135
Hath lost us Heaven, and all this mighty host
In horrible destruction laid thus low,
As far as gods and heavenly essences
Can perish: for the mind and spirit remains
Invincible, and vigour soon returns,   140
Though all our glory extinct, and happy state
Here swallowed up in endless misery.
But what if he our conqueror (whom I now
Of force believe almighty, since no less
Than such could have o'erpowered such force as
          ours)   145
Have left us this our spirit and strength entire,
Strongly to suffer and support our pains,
That we may so suffice his vengeful ire,
Or do him mightier service, as his thralls

By right of war, whate'er his business be,   150
Here in the heart of Hell to work in fire,
Or do his errands in the gloomy deep?
What can it then avail though yet we feel
Strength undiminished, or eternal being,
To undergo eternal punishment?"   155
    Whereto with speedy words the Arch-Fiend replied:
"Fallen Cherub, to be weak is miserable,
Doing or suffering: but of this be sure,
To do aught good never will be our task,
But ever to do ill our sole delight,   160
As being the contrary to his high will
Whom we resist. If then his providence
Out of our evil seek to bring forth good,
Our labour must be to pervert that end,
And out of good still to find means of evil;   165
Which oft times may succeed, so as perhaps
Shall grieve him, if I fail not, and disturb
His inmost counsels from their destined aim.
But see! the angry victor hath recalled
His ministers of vengeance and pursuit   170
Back to the gates of Heaven; the sulphurous hail,
Shot after us in storm, o'erblown hath laid
The fiery surge that from the precipice
Of Heaven received us falling; and the thunder,
Winged with red lightning and impetuous rage,   175
Perhaps hath spent his shafts, and ceases now
To bellow through the vast and boundless deep.
Let us not slip the occasion, whether scorn
Or satiate fury yield it from our foe.
Seest thou yon dreary plain, forlorn and wild,   180
The seat of desolation, void of light,

Save what the glimmering of these livid flames
Casts pale and dreadful? Thither let us tend
From off the tossing of these fiery waves;
There rest, if any rest can harbour there;   185
And, re-assembling our afflicted powers,
Consult how we may henceforth most offend
Our enemy, our own loss how repair,
How overcome this dire calamity,
What reinforcement we may gain from hope,   190
If not what resolution from despair."
    Thus Satan, talking to his nearest mate,
With head uplift above the wave, and eyes
That sparkling blazed; his other parts besides,
Prone on the flood, extended long and large,   195
Lay floating many a rood, in bulk as huge
As whom the fables name of monstrous size,
Titanian, or Earth-born, that warred on Jove,
Briareos or Typhon, whom the den
By ancient Tarsus held, or that sea-beast   200
Leviathan, which God of all his works
Created hugest that swim the ocean stream:
Him haply slumbering on the Norway foam,
The pilot of some small night-foundered skiff
Deeming some island, oft, as seamen tell,   205
With fixed anchor in his scaly rind,
Moors by his side under the lee, while night
Invests the sea, and wished morn delays:
So stretched out huge in length the Arch-Fiend lay,
Chained on the burning lake; nor ever thence   210
Had risen or heaved his head, but that the will
And high permission of all-ruling Heaven
Left him at large to his own dark designs,

That with reiterated crimes he might
Heap on himself damnation, while he sought   215
Evil to others, and enraged might see
How all his malice served but to bring forth
Infinite goodness, grace and mercy shewn
On Man by him seduced, but on himself
Treble confusion, wrath and vengeance poured.   220
   Forthwith upright he rears from off the pool
His mighty stature; on each hand the flames
Driven backward slope their pointing spires, and rolled
In billows, leave i' the midst a horrid vale.
Then with expanded wings he steers his flight   225
Aloft, incumbent on the dusky air,
That felt unusual weight, till on dry land
He lights; if it were land that ever burned
With solid, as the lake with liquid fire,
And such appeared in hue, as when the force   230
Of subterranean wind transports a hill
Torn from Pelorus, or the shattered side
Of thundering Etna, whose combustible
And fuelled entrails thence conceiving fire,
Sublimed with mineral fury, aid the winds,   235
And leave a singed bottom all involved
With stench and smoke: such resting found the sole
Of unblest feet. Him followed his next mate,
Both glorying to have scaped the Stygian flood
As gods and by their own recovered strength,   240
Not by the sufferance of supernal power.
   "Is this the region, this the soil, the clime,"
Said then the lost Archangel, "this the seat
That we must change for Heaven? this mournful
    gloom

For that celestial light? Be it so, since he   245
Who now is sovran can dispose and bid
What shall be right: fardest from him is best,
Whom reason hath equalled, force hath made
    supreme
Above his equals. Farewell happy fields
Where joy for ever dwells; hail, horrors, hail,   250
Infernal world; and thou, profoundest Hell,
Receive thy new possessor, one who brings
A mind not to be changed by place or time.
The mind is its own place, and in itself
Can make a Heaven of Hell, a Hell of Heaven.   255
What matter where, if I be still the same,
And what I should be, all but less than he
Whom thunder hath made greater? Here at least
We shall be free; the Almighty hath not built
Here for his envy, will not drive us hence: 260
Here we may reign secure, and in my choice
To reign is worth ambition, though in Hell:
Better to reign in Hell than serve in Heaven.
But wherefore let we then our faithful friends,
The associates and co-partners of our loss,   265
Lie thus astonished on the oblivious pool,
And call them not to share with us their part
In this unhappy mansion, or once more
With rallied arms to try what may be yet
Regained in Heaven, or what more lost in Hell?"   270
   So Satan spake; and him Beëlzebub
Thus answered: "Leader of those armies bright
Which but the Omnipotent none could have foiled,
If once they hear that voice, their liveliest pledge
Of hope in fears and dangers, heard so oft   275

In worst extremes, and on the perilous edge
Of battle when it raged, in all assaults
Their surest signal, they will soon resume
New courage and revive, though now they lie
Grovelling and prostrate on yon lake of fire,   280
As we erewhile, astounded and amazed;
No wonder, fallen such a pernicious highth!"
    He scarce had ceased when the superior fiend
Was moving toward the shore; his ponderous shield,
Ethereal temper, massy, large, and round,   285
Behind him cast: the broad circumference
Hung on his shoulders like the moon, whose orb
Through optic glass the Tuscan artist views
At evening from the top of Fesole,
Or in Valdarno, to descry new lands,   290
Rivers, or mountains, in her spotty globe.
His spear, to equal which the tallest pine
Hewn on Norwegian hills, to be the mast
Of some great ammiral, were but a wand,
He walked with to support uneasy steps   295
Over the burning marl, not like those steps
On Heaven's azure; and the torrid clime
Smote on him sore besides, vaulted with fire.
Nathless he so endured, till on the beach
Of that inflamèd sea he stood, and called   300
His legions, angel forms, who lay entranced,
Thick as autumnal leaves that strow the brooks
In Vallombrosa, where the Etrurian shades
High over-arched embower; or scattered sedge
Afloat, when with fierce winds Orion armed   305
Hath vexed the Red Sea coast, whose waves o'er-
        threw

Busiris and his Memphian chivalry,
While with perfidious hatred they pursued
The sojourners of Goshen, who beheld
From the safe shore their floating carcases   310
And broken chariot-wheels: so thick bestrown,
Abject and lost, lay these, covering the flood,
Under amazement of their hideous change.
He called so loud that all the hollow deep
Of Hell resounded: "Princes, Potentates,   315
Warriors, the flower of Heaven, once yours, now
        lost,
If such astonishment as this can seize
Eternal spirits; or have ye chosen this place
After the toil of battle to repose
Your wearied virtue, for the ease you find   320
To slumber here, as in the vales of Heaven?
Or in this abject posture have ye sworn
To adore the conqueror, who now beholds
Cherub and Seraph rolling in the flood
With scattered arms and ensigns, till anon   325
His swift pursuers from Heaven-gates discern
The advantage, and descending tread us down
Thus drooping, or with linked thunderbolts
Transfix us to the bottom of this gulf?
Awake, arise, or be for ever fallen!"   330
    They heard, and were abashed, and up they sprung
Upon the wing, as when men wont to watch
On duty, sleeping found by whom they dread,
Rouse and bestir themselves ere well awake.
Nor did they not perceive the evil plight   335
In which they were, or the fierce pains not feel;
Yet to their General's voice they soon obeyed

Innumerable. As when the potent rod
Of Amram's son, in Egypt's evil day,
Waved round the coast, up called a pitchy cloud   340
Of locusts, warping on the eastern wind,
That o'er the realm of impious Pharaoh hung
Like night, and darkened all the land of Nile:
So numberless were those bad angels seen
Hovering on wing under the cope of Hell,   345
'Twixt upper, nether, and surrounding fires;
Till, as a signal given, the uplifted spear
Of their great Sultan waving to direct
Their course, in even balance down they light
On the firm brimstone, and fill all the plain: 350
A multitude, like which the populous North
Poured never from her frozen loins, to pass
Rhene or the Danaw, when her barbarous sons
Came like a deluge on the South, and spread
Beneath Gibraltar to the Libyan sands.   355
Forthwith from every squadron and each band
The heads and leaders thither haste where stood
Their great commander; godlike shapes, and forms
Excelling human, princely dignities,
And powers that erst in Heaven sat on thrones;   360
Though of their names in heavenly records now
Be no memorial, blotted out and rased
By their rebellion from the Books of Life.
Nor had they yet among the sons of Eve
Got them new names, till, wandering o'er the
        Earth,   365
Through God's high sufferance for the trial of man,
  y falsities and lies the greatest part
    mankind they corrupted to forsake

God their creator, and the invisible
Glory of him that made them to transform 370
Oft to the image of a brute, adorned
With gay religions full of pomp and gold,
And devils to adore for deities.
Then were they known to men by various names,
And various idols through the heathen world. 375
   Say, Muse, their names then known, who first,
      who last,
Roused from the slumber on that fiery couch,
At their great emperor's call, as next in worth,
Came singly where he stood on the bare strand,
While the promiscuous crowd stood yet aloof. 380
   The chief were those who, from the pit of Hell
Roaming to seek their prey on Earth, durst fix
Their seats long after next the seat of God,
Their altars by his altar, gods adored
Among the nations round, and durst abide 385
Jehovah thundering out of Sion, throned
Between the Cherubim; yea, often placed
Within his sanctuary itself their shrines,
Abominations; and with cursed things
His holy rites and solemn feasts profaned, 390
And with their darkness durst affront his light.
First Moloch, horrid king, besmeared with blood
Of human sacrifice, and parents' tears,
Though, for the noise of drums and timbrels loud,
Their children's cries unheard, that passed through
     fire 395
To his grim idol. Him the Ammonite
Worshipped in Rabba and her watery plain,
In Argob and in Basan, to the stream

Of utmost Arnon. Nor content with such
Audacious neighbourhood, the wisest heart   400
Of Solomon he led by fraud to build
His temple right against the temple of God
On that opprobrious hill, and made his grove
The pleasant valley of Hinnom, Tophet thence
And black Gehenna called, the type of Hell.   405
Next Chemos, the obscene dread of Moab's sons,
From Aroer to Nebo, and the wild
Of southmost Abarim; in Hesebon
And Horonaim, Seon's realm, beyond
The flowery dale of Sibma clad with vines,   410
And Eleale to the Asphaltic Pool.
Peor his other name, when he enticed
Israel in Sittim on their march from Nile
To do him wanton rites, which cost them woe.
Yet thence his lustful orgies he enlarged   415
Even to that hill of scandal, by the grove
Of Moloch homicide, lust hard by hate;
Till good Josiah drove them thence to Hell.
With these came they who, from the bordering flood
Of old Euphrates to the brook that parts   420
Egypt from Syrian ground, had general names
Of Baalim and Ashtaroth, those male,
These feminine. For Spirits, when they please,
Can either sex assume, or both; so soft
And uncompounded is their essence pure,   425
Not tied or manacled with joint or limb,
Nor founded on the brittle strength of bones,
Like cumbrous flesh; but in what shape they choose
Dilated or condensed, bright or obscure,
Can execute their aery purposes,   430

And works of love or enmity fulfil.
For those the race of Israel oft forsook
Their living Strength, and unfrequented left
His righteous altar, bowing lowly down
To bestial gods; for which their heads as low   435
Bowed down in battle, sunk before the spear
Of despicable foes. With these in troop
Came Astoreth, whom the Phœnicians called
Astarte, Queen of Heaven, with crescent horns;
To whose bright image nightly by the moon   440
Sidonian virgins paid their vows and songs,
In Sion also not unsung, where stood
Her temple on the offensive mountain, built
By that uxorious king whose heart, though large,
Beguiled by fair idolatresses, fell   445
To idols foul. Thammuz came next behind,
Whose annual wound in Lebanon allured
The Syrian damsels to lament his fate
In amorous ditties all a summer's day
While smooth Adonis from his native rock   450
Ran purple to the sea, supposed with blood
Of Thammuz yearly wounded: the love-tale
Infected Sion's daughters with like heat,
Whose wanton passions in the sacred porch
Ezekiel saw, when, by the vision led,   455
His eye surveyed the dark idolatries
Of alienated Judah. Next came one
Who mourned in earnest, when the captive ark
Maimed his brute image, head and hands lopt off
In his own temple, in the grunsel-edge,   460
Where he fell flat, and shamed his worshippers:
Dagon his name, sea-monster, upward man

And downward fish; yet had his temple high
Reared in Azotus, dreaded through the coast
Of Palestine, in Gath and Ascalon,   465
And Accaron and Gaza's frontier bounds.
Him followed Rimmon, whose delightful seat
Was fair Damascus, on the fertile banks
Of Abbana and Pharphar, lucid streams.
He also against the house of God was bold: 470
A leper once he lost and gained a king,
Ahaz, his sottish conqueror, whom he drew
God's altar to disparage and displace
For one of Syrian mode, whereon to burn
His odious offerings, and adore the gods   475
Whom he had vanquished. After these appeared
A crew who, under names of old renown,
Osiris, Isis, Orus, and their train,
With monstrous shapes and sorceries abused
Fanatic Egypt and her priests, to seek   480
Their wandering gods disguised in brutish forms
Rather than human. Nor did Israel scape
The infection, when their borrowed gold composed
The calf in Oreb; and the rebel king
Doubled that sin in Bethel and in Dan,   485
Likening his Maker to the grazed ox,
Jehovah, who, in one night, when he passed
From Egypt marching, equalled with one stroke
Both her first-born and all her bleating gods.
Belial came last, than whom a Spirit more lewd   490
Fell not from Heaven, or more gross to love
Vice for itself: to him no temple stood
Or altar smoked; yet who more oft than he
In temples and at altars, when the priest

Turns atheist? as did Eli's sons, who filled   495
With lust and violence the house of God.
In courts and palaces he also reigns,
And in luxurious cities, where the noise
Of riot ascends above their loftiest towers,
And injury and outrage; and when night   500
Darkens the streets, then wander forth the sons
Of Belial, flown with insolence and wine.
Witness the streets of Sodom, and that night
In Gibeah, when the hospitable door
Exposed a matron, to avoid worse rape.   505
    These were the prime in order and in might;
The rest were long to tell, though far renowned,
The Ionian gods, of Javan's issue held
Gods, yet confessed later than Heaven and Earth,
Their boasted parents: Titan, Heaven's first-born, 510
With his enormous brood, and birthright seized
By younger Saturn; he from mightier Jove,
His own and Rhea's son, like measure found;
So Jove usurping reigned: these first in Crete
And Ida known, thence on the snowy top   515
Of cold Olympus ruled the middle air,
Their highest Heaven; or on the Delphian cliff,
Or in Dodona, and through all the bounds
Of Doric land; or who with Saturn old
Fled over Adria to the Hesperian fields   520
And o'er the Celtic roamed the utmost isles.
    All these and more came flocking; but with looks
Downcast and damp, yet such wherein appeared
Obscure some glimpse of joy, to have found their
    chief
Not in despair, to have found themselves not lost 525

In loss itself; which on his countenance cast
Like doubtful hue: but he, his wonted pride
Soon recollecting, with high words, that bore
Semblance of worth, not substance, gently raised
Their fainting courage, and dispelled their fears: 530
Then straight commands that, at the warlike sound
Of trumpets loud and clarions, be upreared
His mighty standard; that proud honour claimed
Azazel as his right, a Cherub tall:
Who forthwith from the glittering staff unfurled 535
The imperial ensign, which, full high advanced,
Shone like a meteor streaming to the wind,
With gems and golden lustre rich emblazed,
Seraphic arms and trophies; all the while
Sonorous metal blowing martial sounds: 540
At which the universal host up-sent
A shout that tore Hell's concave, and beyond
Frighted the reign of Chaos and old Night.
All in a moment through the gloom were seen
Ten thousand banners rise into the air, 545
With orient colours waving; with them rose
A forest huge of spears; and thronging helms
Appeared, and serried shields in thick array
Of depth immeasurable. Anon they move
In perfect phalanx to the Dorian mood 550
Of flutes and soft recorders; such as raised
To highth of noblest temper heroes old
Arming to battle, and instead of rage
Deliberate valour breathed, firm and unmoved
With dread of death to flight or foul retreat; 555
Nor wanting power to mitigate and wage,
With solemn touches, troubled thoughts, and chase

Anguish and doubt and fear and sorrow and pain
From mortal or immortal minds. Thus they,
Breathing united force with fixed thought, 560
Moved on in silence to soft pipes that charmed
Their painful steps o'er the burnt soil; and now
Advanced in view they stand, a horrid front
Of dreadful length and dazzling arms, in guise
Of warriors old, with ordered spear and shield, 565
Awaiting what command their mighty Chief
Had to impose. He through the armed files
Darts his experienced eye, and soon traverse
The whole battalion views, their order due,
Their visages and stature as of gods; 570
Their number last he sums. And now his heart
Distends with pride, and hardening in his strength
Glories; for never, since created Man,
Met such embodied force as, named with these,
Could merit more than that small infantry 575
Warred on by cranes: though all the giant brood
Of Phlegra with the heroic race were joined
That fought at Thebes and Ilium, on each side
Mixed with auxiliar gods; and what resounds
In fable or romance of Uther's son, 580
Begirt with British and Armoric knights;
And all who since, baptized or infidel,
Jousted in Aspramont, or Montalban,
Damasco, or Marocco, or Trebisond;
Or whom Biserta sent from Afric shore 585
When Charlemain with all his peerage fell
By Fontarabbia. Thus far these beyond
Compare of mortal prowess, yet observed
Their dread Commander: he above the rest

In shape and gesture proudly eminent, 590
Stood like a tower; his form had yet not lost
All her original brightness, nor appeared
Less than archangel ruined, and the excess
Of glory obscured: as when the sun new-risen
Looks through the horizontal misty air 595
Shorn of his beams, or from behind the moon,
In dim eclipse, disastrous twilight sheds
On half the nations, and with fear of change
Perplexes monarchs. Darkened so, yet shone
Above them all the Archangel: but his face 600
Deep scars of thunder had intrenched, and care
Sat on his faded cheek, but under brows
Of dauntless courage, and considerate pride
Waiting revenge: cruel his eye, but cast
Signs of remorse and passion, to behold 605
The fellows of his crime, the followers rather
(Far other once beheld in bliss), condemned
For ever now to have their lot in pain;
Millions of spirits for his fault amerced
Of Heaven, and from eternal splendours flung 610
For his revolt; yet faithful how they stood,
Their glory withered: as, when Heaven's fire
Hath scathed the forest oaks or mountain pines,
With singed top their stately growth, though bare,
Stands on the blasted heath. He now prepared 615
To speak; whereat their doubled ranks they bend
From wing to wing, and half enclose him round
With all his peers: attention held them mute.
Thrice he assayed, and thrice in spite of scorn
Tears, such as angels weep, burst forth: at last 620
Words interwove with sighs found out their way:

"O myriads of immortal spirits, O Powers
Matchless but with the Almighty—and that strife
Was not inglorious, though the event was dire,
As this place testifies, and this dire change,   625
Hateful to utter—but what power of mind,
Foreseeing or presaging, from the depth
Of knowledge past or present, could have feared
How such united force of gods, how such
As stood like these, could ever know repulse?   630
For who can yet believe, though after loss,
That all these puissant legions, whose exile
Hath emptied Heaven, shall fail to re-ascend,
Self-raised, and re-possess their native seat?
For me, be witness all the host of Heaven,   635
If counsels different, or danger shunned
By me, have lost our hopes. But he who reigns
Monarch in Heaven, till then as one secure
Sat on his throne, upheld by old repute,
Consent or custom, and his regal state   640
Put forth at full, but still his strength concealed,
Which tempted our attempt, and wrought our fall.
Henceforth his might we know, and know our own,
So as not either to provoke, or dread
New war, provoked; our better part remains   645
To work in close design, by fraud or guile,
What force effected not; that he no less
At length from us may find, who overcomes
By force hath overcome but half his foe.
Space may produce new worlds; whereof so rife   650
There went a fame in Heaven that he ere long
Intended to create, and therein plant
A generation whom his choice regard

Should favour equal to the sons of Heaven.
Thither, if but to pry, shall be perhaps   655
Our first eruption, thither or elsewhere;
For this infernal pit shall never hold
Celestial spirits in bondage, nor the Abyss
Long under darkness cover. But these thoughts
Full counsel must mature: peace is despaired,   660
For who can think submission? War, then, war
Open or understood, must be resolved."

He spake; and to confirm his words, out-flew
Millions of flaming swords, drawn from the thighs
Of mighty Cherubim; the sudden blaze   665
Far round illumined Hell: highly they raged
Against the Highest, and fierce with grasped arms
Clashed on their sounding shields the din of war,
Hurling defiance toward the vault of Heaven.

There stood a hill not far, whose grisly top   670
Belched fire and rolling smoke; the rest entire
Shone with a glossy scurf, undoubted sign
That in his womb was hid metallic ore,
The work of sulphur. Thither, winged with speed,
A numerous brigad hastened: as when bands   675
Of pioners, with spade and pickaxe armed,
Forerun the royal camp, to trench a field
Or cast a rampart. Mammon led them on,
Mammon, the least erected spirit that fell
From Heaven, for even in Heaven his looks and
          thoughts   680
Were always downward bent, admiring more
The riches of Heaven's pavement, trodden gold,
Than aught divine or holy else enjoyed
In vision beatific. By him first

Men also, and by his suggestion taught,   685
Ransacked the centre, and with impious hands
Rifled the bowels of their mother Earth
For treasures better hid. Soon had his crew
Opened into the hill a spacious wound
And digged out ribs of gold. Let none admire   690
That riches grow in Hell; that soil may best
Deserve the precious bane. And here let those
Who boast in mortal things, and wondering tell
Of Babel, and the works of Memphian kings,
Learn how their greatest monuments of fame   695
And strength and art are easily outdone
By spirits reprobate, and in an hour
What in an age they with incessant toil
And hands innumerable scarce perform.
Nigh on the plain, in many cells prepared,   700
That underneath had veins of liquid fire
Sluiced from the lake, a second multitude
With wondrous art founded the massy ore,
Severing each kind, and scummed the bullion dross:
A third as soon had formed within the ground   705
A various mould, and from the boiling cells
By strange conveyance filled each hollow nook;
As in an organ from one blast of wind
To many a row of pipes the sound-board breathes.
Anon out of the earth a fabric huge   710
Rose like an exhalation, with the sound
Of dulcet symphonies and voices sweet,
Built like a temple, where pilasters round
Were set, and Doric pillars overlaid
With golden architrave; nor did there want   715
Cornice or frieze, with bossy sculptures graven;

The roof was fretted gold. Not Babylon,
Nor great Alcairo, such magnificence
Equalled in all their glories, to enshrine
Belus or Serapis their gods, or seat   720
Their kings, when Egypt with Assyria strove
In wealth and luxury. The ascending pile
Stood fixed her stately highth, and straight the doors,
Opening their brazen folds, discover, wide
Within, her ample spaces o'er the smooth   725
And level pavement: from the arched roof,
Pendent by subtle magic, many a row
Of starry lamps and blazing cressets, fed
With naphtha and asphaltus, yielded light
As from a sky. The hasty multitude   730
Admiring entered, and the work some praise,
And some the architect: his hand was known
In Heaven by many a towered structure high,
Where sceptred angels held their residence,
And sat as princes, whom the supreme King   735
Exalted to such power, and gave to rule,
Each in his hierarchy, the orders bright.
Nor was his name unheard or unadored
In ancient Greece; and in Ausonian land
Men called him Mulciber; and how he fell   740
From Heaven they fabled, thrown by angry Jove
Sheer o'er the crystal battlements: from morn
To noon he fell, from noon to dewy eve,
A summer's day; and with the setting sun
Dropt from the zenith like a falling star   745
On Lemnos, the Ægæan isle. Thus they relate,
Erring; for he with this rebellious rout
Fell long before; nor aught availed him now

To have built in Heaven high towers; nor did he
    scape
By all his engines, but was headlong sent   750
With his industrous crew to build in Hell.
   Meanwhile the winged haralds, by command
Of sovran power, with awful ceremony
And trumpet's sound, throughout the host proclaim
A solemn council forthwith to be held   755
At Pandemonium, the high capital
Of Satan and his peers: their summons called
From every band and squared regiment
By place or choice the worthiest; they anon
With hundreds and with thousands trooping came 760
Attended. All access was thronged, the gates
And porches wide, but chief the spacious hall
(Though like a covered field, where champions bold
Wont ride in armed, and at the Soldan's chair
Defied the best of Panim chivalry   765
To mortal combat, or career with lance)
Thick swarmed, both on the ground and in the air,
Brushed with the hiss of rustling wings. As bees
In spring-time, when the Sun with Taurus rides,
Pour forth their populous youth about the hive   770
In clusters; they among fresh dews and flowers
Fly to and fro, or on the smoothed plank,
The suburb of their straw-built citadel,
New rubbed with balm, expatiate and confer
Their state-affairs. So thick the aery crowd   775
Swarmed and were straitened; till the signal given,
Behold a wonder! they but now who seemed
In bigness to surpass Earth's giant sons,
Now less than smallest dwarfs, in narrow room

Throng numberless, like that pygmean race   780
Beyond the Indian mount; or faery elves,
Whose midnight revels by a forest-side
Or fountain some belated peasant sees,
Or dreams he sees, while overhead the moon
Sits arbitress, and nearer to the earth   785
Wheels her pale course; they, on their mirth and
     dance
Intent, with jocund music charm his ear;
At once with joy and fear his heart rebounds.
Thus incorporeal spirits to smallest forms
Reduced their shapes immense, and were at large,   790
Though without number still, amidst the hall
Of that infernal court. But far within,
And in their own dimensions like themselves,
The great Seraphic Lords and Cherubim
In close recess and secret conclave sat,   795
A thousand demi-gods on golden seats,
Frequent and full. After short silence then
And summons read, the great consult began.

PARADISE LOST

Book II

High on a throne of royal state, which far
Outshone the wealth of Ormus and of Ind,
Or where the gorgeous East with richest hand
Showers on her kings barbaric pearl and gold,
Satan exalted sat, by merit raised   5
To that bad eminence; and, from despair
Thus high uplifted beyond hope, aspires
Beyond thus high, insatiate to pursue
Vain war with Heaven; and, by success untaught,
His proud imaginations thus displayed: 10
    "Powers and Dominions, deities of Heaven!
For since no deep within her gulf can hold
Immortal vigour, though oppressed and fallen,
I give not Heaven for lost. From this descent
Celestial Virtues rising will appear   15
More glorious and more dread than from no fall,
And trust themselves to fear no second fate.
Me though just right, and the fixed laws of Heaven,
Did first create your leader, next, free choice,
With what besides, in counsel or in fight,   20
Hath been achieved of merit, yet this loss,
Thus far at least recovered, hath much more
Established in a safe unenvied throne,

Yielded with full consent. The happier state
In Heaven which follows dignity might draw   25
Envy from each inferior; but who here
Will envy whom the highest place exposes
Foremost to stand against the Thunderer's aim
Your bulwark, and condemns to greatest share
Of endless pain? Where there is then no good   30
For which to strive, no strife can grow up there
From faction; for none sure will claim in Hell
Precedence, none whose portion is so small
Of present pain that with ambitious mind
Will covet more. With this advantage then   35
To union and firm faith and firm accord,
More than can be in Heaven, we now return
To claim our just inheritance of old,
Surer to prosper than prosperity
Could have assured us; and by what best way,   40
Whether of open war or covert guile,
We now debate; who can advise may speak."

    He ceased; and next him Moloch, sceptred king,
Stood up, the strongest and the fiercest spirit
That fought in Heaven, now fiercer by despair: 45
His trust was with the Eternal to be deemed
Equal in strength, and rather than be less
Cared not to be at all; with that care lost
Went all his fear: of God, or Hell, or worse,
He recked not, and these words thereafter spake: 50

    "My sentence is for open war: of wiles,
More unexpert, I boast not: them let those
Contrive who need, or when they need, not now.
For while they sit contriving, shall the rest,
Millions that stand in arms, and longing wait   55

The signal to ascend, sit lingering here
Heaven's fugitives, and for their dwelling-place
Accept this dark opprobrious den of shame,
The prison of his tyranny who reigns
By our delay? No, let us rather choose,   60
Armed with hell-flames and fury, all at once
O'er Heaven's high towers to force resistless way,
Turning our tortures into horrid arms
Against the torturer; when to meet the noise
Of his almighty engine he shall hear   65
Infernal thunder, and for lightning see
Black fire and horror shot with equal rage
Among his angels, and his throne itself
Mixed with Tartarean sulphur and strange fire,
His own invented torments. But perhaps   70
The way seems difficult and steep to scale
With upright wing against a higher foe.
Let such bethink them, if the sleepy drench
Of that forgetful lake benumb not still,
That in our proper motion we ascend   75
Up to our native seat; descent and fall
To us is adverse. Who but felt of late,
When the fierce foe hung on our broken rear
Insulting, and pursued us through the Deep,
With what compulsion and laborious flight   80
We sunk thus low? The ascent is easy then;
The event is feared: should we again provoke
Our stronger, some worse way his wrath may find
To our destruction, if there be in Hell
Fear to be worse destroyed. What can be worse   85
Than to dwell here, driven out from bliss, condemned
In his abhorrèd deep to utter woe;

Where pain of unextinguishable fire
Must exercise us without hope of end,
The vassals of his anger, when the scourge   90
Inexorably and the torturing hour
Calls us to penance? More destroyed than thus,
We should be quite abolished and expire.
What fear we then? what doubt we to incense
His utmost ire? which, to the highth enraged,   95
Will either quite consume us, and reduce
To nothing this essential, happier far
Than miserable to have eternal being;
Or if our substance be indeed divine,
And cannot cease to be, we are at worst   100
On this side nothing; and by proof we feel
Our power sufficient to disturb his Heaven,
And with perpetual inroads to alarm,
Though inaccessible, his fatal throne:
Which, if not victory, is yet revenge."   105
    He ended frowning, and his look denounced
Desperate revenge, and battle dangerous
To less than gods. On the other side up rose
Belial, in act more graceful and humane;
A fairer person lost not Heaven; he seemed   110
For dignity composed, and high exploit:
But all was false and hollow; though his tongue
Dropt manna, and could make the worse appear
The better reason, to perplex and dash
Maturest counsels: for his thoughts were low;   115
To vice industrious, but to nobler deeds
Timorous and slothful: yet he pleased the ear,
And with persuasive accent thus began:
    "I should be much for open war, O peers,

As not behind in hate, if what was urged   120
Main reason to persuade immediate war
Did not dissuade me most, and seem to cast
Ominous conjecture on the whole success;
When he who most excels in fact of arms,
In what he counsels and in what excels   125
Mistrustful, grounds his courage on despair
And utter dissolution, as the scope
Of all his aim, after some dire revenge.
First, what revenge? The towers of Heaven are filled
With armed watch, that render all access   130
Impregnable; oft on the bordering Deep
Encamp their legions, or with obscure wing
Scout far and wide into the realm of Night,
Scorning surprise. Or could we break our way
By force, and at our heels all Hell should rise   135
With blackest insurrection, to confound
Heaven's purest light, yet our great enemy
All incorruptible would on his throne
Sit unpolluted, and the ethereal mould
Incapable of stain would soon expel   140
Her mischief, and purge off the baser fire,
Victorious. Thus repulsed, our final hope
Is flat despair; we must exasperate
The almighty victor to spend all his rage,
And that must end us, that must be our cure: 145
To be no more. Sad cure; for who would lose,
Though full of pain, this intellectual being,
Those thoughts that wander through eternity,
To perish rather, swallowed up and lost
In the wide womb of uncreated Night,   150
Devoid of sense and motion? And who knows,

Let this be good, whether our angry foe
Can give it, or will ever? how he can
Is doubtful: that he never will is sure.
Will he, so wise, let loose at once his ire,   155
Belike through impotence, or unaware,
To give his enemies their wish, and end
Them in his anger, whom his anger saves
To punish endless? 'Wherefore cease we, then?'
Say they who counsel war; 'we are decreed,   160
Reserved, and destined to eternal woe;
Whatever doing, what can we suffer more,
What can we suffer worse?' Is this then worst,
Thus sitting, thus consulting, thus in arms?
What when we fled amain, pursued and strook   165
With Heaven's afflicting thunder, and besought
The deep to shelter us? this Hell then seemed
A refuge from those wounds; or when we lay
Chained on the burning lake? that sure was worse.
What if the breath that kindled those grim fires,   170
Awaked, should blow them into sevenfold rage
And plunge us in the flames? or from above
Should intermitted vengeance arm again
His red right hand to plague us? what if all
Her stores were opened, and this firmament   175
Of Hell should spout her cataracts of fire,
Impendent horrors, threatening hideous fall
One day upon our heads; while we perhaps,
Designing or exhorting glorious war,
Caught in a fiery tempest shall be hurled,   180
Each on his rock transfixed, the sport and prey
Of racking whirlwinds, or for ever sunk
Under yon boiling ocean, wrapt in chains;

There to converse with everlasting groans,
Unrespited, unpitied, unreprieved,   185
Ages of hopeless end: this would be worse.
War therefore, open or concealed, alike
My voice dissuades; for what can force or guile
With him, or who deceive his mind, whose eye
Views all things at one view? He from Heaven's
      highth   190
All these our motions vain sees and derides,
Not more almighty to resist our might
Than wise to frustrate all our plots and wiles.
Shall we then live thus vile, the race of Heaven
Thus trampled, thus expelled to suffer here   195
Chains and these torments? Better these than worse,
By my advice; since fate inevitable
Subdues us, and omnipotent decree,
The victor's will. To suffer, as to do,
Our strength is equal, nor the law unjust   200
That so ordains: this was at first resolved,
If we were wise, against so great a foe
Contending, and so doubtful what might fall.
I laugh, when those who at the spear are bold
And vent'rous, if that fail them, shrink, and fear   205
What yet they know must follow: to endure
Exile, or ignominy, or bonds, or pain,
The sentence of their conqueror. This is now
Our doom; which if we can sustain and bear,
Our supreme foe in time may much remit   210
His anger, and perhaps thus far removed
Not mind us not offending, satisfied
With what is punished; whence these raging fires
Will slacken, if his breath stir not their flames.

Our purer essence then will overcome   215
Their noxious vapour, or inured not feel,
Or changed at length and to the place conformed
In temper and in nature, will receive
Familiar the fierce heat, and void of pain;
This horror will grow mild, this darkness light;   220
Besides what hope the never-ending flight
Of future days may bring, what chance, what change
Worth waiting, since our present lot appears
For happy though but ill, for ill not worst,
If we procure not to ourselves more woe."   225
    Thus Belial, with words clothed in reason's garb,
Counselled ignoble ease, and peaceful sloth,
Not peace; and after him thus Mammon spake:
    "Either to disenthrone the King of Heaven
We war, if war be best, or to regain   230
Our own right lost: him to unthrone we then
May hope, when everlasting Fate shall yield
To fickle Chance, and Chaos judge the strife.
The former, vain to hope, argues as vain
The latter; for what place can be for us   235
Within Heaven's bound, unless Heaven's Lord
        supreme
We overpower? Suppose he should relent
And publish grace to all, on promise made
Of new subjection; with what eyes could we
Stand in his presence humble, and receive   240
Strict laws imposed, to celebrate his throne
With warbled hymns, and to his Godhead sing
Forced halleluiahs; while he lordly sits
Our envied sovran, and his altar breathes
Ambrosial odours and ambrosial flowers,   245

Our servile offerings? This must be our task
In Heaven, this our delight; how wearisome
Eternity so spent in worship paid
To whom we hate! Let us not then pursue,
By force impossible, by leave obtained   250
Unacceptable, though in Heaven, our state
Of splendid vassalage; but rather seek
Our own good from ourselves, and from our own
Live to ourselves, though in this vast recess,
Free, and to none accountable, preferring   255
Hard liberty before the easy yoke
Of servile pomp. Our greatness will appear
Then most conspicuous, when great things of small,
Useful of hurtful, prosperous of adverse,
We can create, and in what place soe'er   260
Thrive under evil, and work ease out of pain
Through labour and endurance. This deep world
Of darkness do we dread? How oft amidst
Thick clouds and dark doth Heaven's all-ruling Sire
Choose to reside, his glory unobscured,   265
And with the majesty of darkness round
Covers his throne, from whence deep thunders roar
Mustering their rage, and Heaven resembles Hell!
As he our darkness, cannot we his light
Imitate when we please? This desert soil   270
Wants not her hidden lustre, gems and gold;
Nor want we skill or art, from whence to raise
Magnificence; and what can Heaven show more?
Our torments also may in length of time
Become our elements, these piercing fires   275
As soft as now severe, our temper changed
Into their temper; which must needs remove

The sensible of pain. All things invite
To peaceful counsels, and the settled state
Of order, how in safety best we may   280
Compose our present evils, with regard
Of what we are and were, dismissing quite
All thoughts of war. Ye have what I advise."

    He scarce had finished, when such murmur filled
The assembly, as when hollow rocks retain   285
The sound of blustering winds, which all night long
Had roused the sea, now with hoarse cadence lull
Seafaring men o'erwatched, whose bark by chance,
Or pinnace, anchors in a craggy bay
After the tempest: such applause was heard   290
As Mammon ended, and his sentence pleased,
Advising peace; for such another field
They dreaded worse than Hell; so much the fear
Of thunder and the sword of Michaël
Wrought still within them; and no less desire   295
To found this neither empire, which might rise,
By policy and long process of time,
In emulation opposite to Heaven.
Which when Beëlzebub perceived, than whom,
Satan except, none higher sat, with grave   300
Aspect he rose, and in his rising seemed
A pillar of state; deep on his front engraven
Deliberation sat and public care;
And princely counsel in his face yet shone,
Majestic though in ruin: sage he stood,   305
With Atlantean shoulders fit to bear
The weight of mightiest monarchies; his look
Drew audience and attention still as night
Or summer's noontide air, while thus he spake:

"Thrones and imperial Powers, offspring of
    Heaven, 310
Ethereal Virtues—or these titles now
Must we renounce, and, changing style, be called
Princes of Hell? for so the popular vote
Inclines, here to continue, and build up here
A growing empire; doubtless! while we dream, 315
And know not that the King of Heaven hath doomed
This place our dungeon, not our safe retreat
Beyond his potent arm, to live exempt
From Heaven's high jurisdiction, in new league
Banded against his throne, but to remain 320
In strictest bondage, though thus far removed,
Under the inevitable curb, reserved
His captive multitude. For he, be sure,
In highth or depth, still first and last will reign
Sole king, and of his kingdom lose no part 325
By our revolt, but over Hell extend
His empire, and with iron sceptre rule
Us here, as with his golden those in Heaven.
What sit we then projecting peace and war?
War hath determined us, and foiled with loss 330
Irreparable; terms of peace yet none
Voutsafed or sought; for what peace will be given
To us enslaved, but custody severe,
And stripes, and arbitrary punishment
Inflicted? and what peace can we return, 335
But to our power hostility and hate,
Untamed reluctance, and revenge, though slow,
Yet ever plotting how the conqueror least
May reap his conquest, and may least rejoice
In doing what we most in suffering feel? 340

Nor will occasion want, nor shall we need
With dangerous expedition to invade
Heaven, whose high walls fear no assault or siege,
Or ambush from the deep. What if we find
Some easier enterprise? There is a place   345
(If ancient and prophetic fame in Heaven
Err not), another world, the happy seat
Of some new race called Man, about this time
To be created like to us, though less
In power and excellence, but favoured more   350
Of him who rules above; so was his will
Pronounced among the gods, and by an oath,
That shook Heaven's whole circumference, confirmed
Thither let us bend all our thoughts, to learn
What creatures there inhabit, of what mould   355
Or substance, how endued, and what their power,
And where their weakness, how attempted best,
By force or subtlety. Though Heaven be shut,
And Heaven's high Arbitrator sit secure
In his own strength, this place may lie exposed,   360
The utmost border of his kingdom, left
To their defence who hold it; here perhaps
Some advantageous act may be achieved
By sudden onset: either with Hell-fire
To waste his whole creation, or possess   365
All as our own, and drive, as we are driven,
The puny habitants; or if not drive,
Seduce them to our party, that their God
May prove their foe, and with repenting hand
Abolish his own works. This would surpass   370
Common revenge, and interrupt his joy
In our confusion, and our joy upraise

In his disturbance; when his darling sons,
Hurled headlong to partake with us, shall curse
Their frail original, and faded bliss,   375
Faded so soon. Advise if this be worth
Attempting, or to sit in darkness here
Hatching vain empires." Thus Beëlzebub
Pleaded his devilish counsel, first devised
By Satan, and in part proposed; for whence,   380
But from the author of all ill, could spring
So deep a malice, to confound the race
Of mankind in one root, and Earth with Hell
To mingle and involve, done all to spite
The great Creator? But their spite still serves   385
His glory to augment. The bold design
Pleased highly those infernal States, and joy
Sparkled in all their eyes; with full assent
They vote: whereat his speech he thus renews:
    "Well have ye judged, well ended long debate, 390
Synod of gods, and, like to what ye are,
Great things resolved; which from the lowest deep
Will once more lift us up, in spite of fate,
Nearer our ancient seat; perhaps in view
Of those bright confines, whence, with neighbouring
        arms   395
And opportune excursion, we may chance
Re-enter Heaven; or else in some mild zone
Dwell not unvisited of Heaven's fair light,
Secure, and at the brightening orient beam
Purge off this gloom; the soft delicious air,   400
To heal the scar of these corrosive fires,
Shall breathe her balm. But first, whom shall we send
In search of this new world? whom shall we find

Sufficient? who shall tempt with wandering feet
The dark, unbottomed, infinite Abyss,   405
And through the palpable obscure find out
His uncouth way, or spread his aery flight,
Upborne with indefatigable wings
Over the vast abrupt, ere he arrive
The happy isle? what strength, what art, can then 410
Suffice, or what evasion bear him safe
Through the strict senteries and stations thick
Of angels watching round? Here he had need
All circumspection, and we now no less
Choice in our suffrage; for on whom we send   415
The weight of all and our last hope relies."

    This said, he sat; and expectation held
His look suspense, awaiting who appeared
To second, or oppose, or undertake
The perilous attempt: but all sat mute,   420
Pondering the danger with deep thoughts; and each
In other's countenance read his own dismay,
Astonished. None among the choice and prime
Of those heaven-warring champions could be found
So hardy as to proffer or accept,   425
Alone, the dreadful voyage; till at last
Satan, whom now transcendent glory raised
Above his fellows, with monarchal pride
Conscious of highest worth, unmoved thus spake:

    "O progeny of Heaven, empyreal Thrones!   430
With reason hath deep silence and demur
Seized us, though undismayed: long is the way
And hard, that out of Hell leads up to light;
Our prison strong, this huge convex of fire,
Outrageous to devour, immures us round   435

Ninefold, and gates of burning adamant,
Barred over us, prohibit all egress.
These passed, if any pass, the void profound
Of unessential night receives him next,
Wide-gaping, and with utter loss of being   440
Threatens him, plunged in that abortive gulf.
If thence he scape into whatever world
Or unknown region, what remains him less
Than unknown dangers and as hard escape?
But I should ill become this throne, O peers   445
And this imperial sovranty, adorned
With splendour, armed with power, if aught proposed
And judged of public moment, in the shape
Of difficulty or danger, could deter
Me from attempting. Wherefore do I assume   450
These royalties, and not refuse to reign,
Refusing to accept as great a share
Of hazard as of honour, due alike
To him who reigns, and so much to him due
Of hazard more, as he above the rest   455
High honoured sits? Go therefore, mighty Powers,
Terror of Heaven, though fallen; intend at home,
While here shall be our home, what best may ease
The present misery, and render Hell
More tolerable; if there be cure or charm   460
To respite, or deceive, or slack the pain
Of this ill mansion; intermit no watch
Against a wakeful foe, while I abroad
Through all the coasts of dark destruction seek
Deliverance for us all: this enterprise   465
None shall partake with me." Thus saying, rose
The monarch, and prevented all reply;

Prudent, lest, from his resolution raised,
Others among the chief might offer now
(Certain to be refused) what erst they feared,   470
And, so refused, might in opinion stand
His rivals, winning cheap the high repute
Which he through hazard huge must earn. But they
Dreaded not more the adventure than his voice
Forbidding; and at once with him they rose;   475
Their rising all at once was as the sound
Of thunder heard remote. Towards him they bend
With awful reverence prone; and as a god
Extol him equal to the Highest in Heaven.
Nor failed they to express how much they praised 480
That for the general safety he despised
His own; for neither do the spirits damned
Lose all their virtue; lest bad men should boast
Their specious deeds on Earth, which glory excites,
Or close ambition varnished o'er with zeal.   485
   Thus they their doubtful consultations dark
Ended, rejoicing in their matchless chief:
As when from mountain-tops the dusky clouds
Ascending, while the north wind sleeps, o'erspread
Heaven's cheerful face, the louring element   490
Scowls o'er the darkened landskip snow or shower;
If chance the radiant sun with farewell sweet
Extend his evening beam, the fields revive,
The birds their notes renew, and bleating herds
Attest their joy, that hill and valley rings.   495
O shame to men! Devil with devil damned
Firm concord holds, men only disagree
Of creatures rational, though under hope
Of heavenly grace; and, God proclaiming peace,

Yet live in hatred, enmity, and strife   500
Among themselves, and levy cruel wars,
Wasting the earth each other to destroy:
As if (which might induce us to accord)
Man had not hellish foes enow besides,
That day and night for his destruction wait.   505
  The Stygian council thus dissolved; and forth
In order came the grand infernal peers;
Midst came their mighty paramount, and seemed
Alone the antagonist of Heaven, nor less
Than Hell's dread emperor, with pomp supreme, 510
And god-like imitated state; him round
A globe of fiery Seraphim enclosed
With bright emblazonry and horrent arms.
Then of their session ended they bid cry
With trumpets' regal sound the great result: 515
Toward the four winds four speedy Cherubim
Put to their mouths the sounding alchymy,
By harald's voice explained; the hollow abyss
Heard far and wide, and all the host of Hell
With deafening shout returned them loud acclaim. 520
Thence more at ease their minds and somewhat raised
By false presumptuous hope, the ranged powers
Disband; and, wandering, each his several way
Pursues, as inclination or sad choice
Leads him perplexed, where he may likeliest find 525
Truce to his restless thoughts, and entertain
The irksome hours, till this great chief return.
Part on the plain or in the air sublime
Upon the wing or in swift race contend,
As at the Olympian games or Pythian fields;   530
Part curb their fiery steeds, or shun the goal

With rapid wheels, or fronted brigads form:
As when, to warn proud cities, war appears
Waged in the troubled sky, and armies rush
To battle in the clouds; before each van   535
Prick forth the aery knights, and couch their spears,
Till thickest legions close; with feats of arms
From either end of heaven the welkin burns.
Others, with vast Typhœan rage more fell,
Rend up both rocks and hills, and ride the air   540
In whirlwind; Hell scarce holds the wild uproar:
As when Alcides, from Oechalia crowned
With conquest, felt the envenomed robe, and tore
Through pain up by the roots Thessalian pines,
And Lichas from the top of Oeta threw   545
Into the Euboic sea. Others more mild,
Retreated in a silent valley, sing
With notes angelical to many a harp
Their own heroic deeds and hapless fall
By doom of battle; and complain that fate   550
Free virtue should enthrall to force or chance.
Their song was partial, but the harmony
(What could it less when spirits immortal sing?)
Suspended Hell, and took with ravishment
The thronging audience. In discourse more sweet   555
(For eloquence the soul, song charms the sense)
Others apart sat on a hill retired,
In thoughts more elevate, and reasoned high
Of providence, foreknowledge, will, and fate,
Fixed fate, free will, foreknowledge absolute,   560
And found no end, in wandering mazes lost.
Of good and evil much they argued then,
Of happiness and final misery,

Passion and apathy, and glory and shame,
Vain wisdom all, and false philosophy;   565
Yet with a pleasing sorcery could charm
Pain for a while or anguish, and excite
Fallacious hope, or arm the obdured breast
With stubborn patience as with triple steel.
Another part, in squadrons and gross bands,   570
On bold adventure to discover wide
That dismal world, if any clime perhaps
Might yield them easier habitation, bend
Four ways their flying march, along the banks
Of four infernal rivers that disgorge   575
Into the burning lake their baleful streams:
Abhorred Styx, the flood of deadly hate;
Sad Acheron of sorrow, black and deep;
Cocytus, named of lamentation loud
Heard on the rueful stream; fierce Phlegethon,   580
Whose waves of torrent fire inflame with rage.
Far off from these a slow and silent stream,
Lethe, the river of oblivion, rolls
Her watery labyrinth, whereof who drinks
Forthwith his former state and being forgets,   585
Forgets both joy and grief, pleasure and pain.
Beyond this flood a frozen continent
Lies dark and wild, beat with perpetual storms
Of whirlwind and dire hail, which on firm land
Thaws not, but gathers heap, and ruin seems   590
Of ancient pile; all else deep snow and ice,
A gulf profound as that Serbonian bog
Betwixt Damiata and Mount Casius old,
Where armies whole have sunk: the parching air
Burns frore, and cold performs the effect of fire.   595

Thither, by harpy-footed Furies haled,
At certain revolutions all the damned
Are brought; and feel by turns the bitter change
Of fierce extremes, extremes by change more fierce,
From beds of raging fire to starve in ice   600
Their soft ethereal warmth, and there to pine
Immovable, infixed, and frozen round
Periods of time; thence hurried back to fire.
They ferry over this Lethean sound
Both to and fro, their sorrow to augment,   605
And wish and struggle, as they pass, to reach
The tempting stream, with one small drop to lose
In sweet forgetfulness all pain and woe,
All in one moment, and so near the brink;
But Fate withstands, and, to oppose the attempt, 610
Medusa with Gorgonian terror guards
The ford, and of itself the water flies
All taste of living wight, as once it fled
The lip of Tantalus. Thus roving on
In confused march forlorn, the adventurous
        bands,   615
With shuddering horror pale, and eyes aghast,
Viewed first their lamentable lot, and found
No rest: through many a dark and dreary vale
They passed, and many a region dolorous,
O'er many a frozen, many a fiery alp,   620
Rocks, caves, lakes, fens, bogs, dens, and shades of
        death,
A universe of death, which God by curse
Created evil, for evil only good,
Where all life dies, death lives, and Nature breeds,
Perverse, all monstrous, all prodigious things,   625

Abominable, inutterable, and worse
Than fables yet have feigned, or fear conceived,
Gorgons, and Hydras, and Chimæras dire.
 Meanwhile the Adversary of God and Man,
Satan, with thoughts inflamed of highest design,   630
Puts on swift wings, and toward the gates of Hell
Explores his solitary flight; sometimes
He scours the right hand coast, sometimes the left;
Now shaves with level wing the deep, then soars
Up to the fiery concave towering high.   635
As when far off at sea a fleet descried
Hangs in the clouds, by equinoctial winds
Close sailing from Bengala, or the isles
Of Ternate and Tidore, whence merchants bring
Their spicy drugs; they on the trading flood   640
Through the wide Ethiopian to the Cape
Ply stemming nightly toward the pole: so seemed
Far off the flying Fiend. At last appear
Hell-bounds, high reaching to the horrid roof,
And thrice threefold the gates; three folds were
        brass,   645
Three iron, three of adamantine rock,
Impenetrable, impaled with circling fire,
Yet unconsumed. Before the gates there sat
On either side a formidable shape.
The one seemed woman to the waist, and fair,   650
But ended foul in many a scaly fold
Voluminous and vast, a serpent armed
With mortal sting: about her middle round
A cry of hell-hounds never ceasing barked
With wide Cerberean mouths full loud, and rung   655
A hideous peal; yet, when they list, would creep,

If aught disturbed their noise, into her womb,
And kennel there, yet there still barked and howled
Within unseen. Far less abhorred than these
Vexed Scylla, bathing in the sea that parts   660
Calabria from the hoarse Trinacrian shore;
Nor uglier follow the night-hag, when, called
In secret, riding through the air she comes,
Lured with the smell of infant blood, to dance
With Lapland witches, while the labouring moon 665
Eclipses at their charms. The other shape—
If shape it might be called that shape had none
Distinguishable in member, joint, or limb;
Or substance might be called that shadow seemed,
For each seemed either—black it stood as night, 670
Fierce as ten Furies, terrible as Hell,
And shook a dreadful dart; what seemed his head
The likeness of a kingly crown had on.
Satan was now at hand, and from his seat
The monster moving onward came as fast   675
With horrid strides; Hell trembled as he strode.
The undaunted Fiend what this might be admired,
Admired, not feared—God and his Son except,
Created thing naught valued he nor shunned—
And with disdainful look thus first began: 680
    "Whence and what art thou, execrable shape,
That dar'st, though grim and terrible, advance
Thy miscreated front athwart my way
To yonder gates? Through them I mean to pass,
That be assured, without leave asked of thee.   685
Retire, or taste thy folly, and learn by proof,
Hell-born, not to contend with spirits of Heaven."
    To whom the goblin, full of wrath, replied:

"Art thou that traitor angel, art thou he,
Who first broke peace in Heaven and faith, till
    then   690
Unbroken, and in proud rebellious arms
Drew after him the third part of Heaven's sons,
Conjured against the Highest, for which both thou
And they, outcast from God, are here condemned
To waste eternal days in woe and pain?   695
And reckon'st thou thyself with spirits of Heaven,
Hell-doomed, and breath'st defiance here and scorn,
Where I reign king, and, to enrage thee more,
Thy king and lord? Back to thy punishment,
False fugitive, and to thy speed add wings,   700
Lest with a whip of scorpions I pursue
Thy lingering, or with one stroke of this dart
Strange horror seize thee, and pangs unfelt before."
    So spake the grisly terror, and in shape,
So speaking and so threatening, grew tenfold   705
More dreadful and deform: on the other side,
Incensed with indignation, Satan stood
Unterrified, and like a comet burned,
That fires the length of Ophiuchus huge
In the artic sky, and from his horrid hair   710
Shakes pestilence and war. Each at the head
Levelled his deadly aim; their fatal hands
No second stroke intend; and such a frown
Each cast at the other, as when two black clouds,
With Heaven's artillery fraught, come rattling on 715
Over the Caspian, then stand front to front
Hovering a space, till winds the signal blow
To join their dark encounter in mid air:
So frowned the mighty combatants, that Hell

Grew darker at their frown; so matched they
    stood; 720
For never but once more was either like
To meet so great a foe. And now great deeds
Had been achieved, whereof all Hell had rung,
Had not the snaky sorceress, that sat
Fast by Hell-gate and kept the fatal key, 725
Risen, and with hideous outcry rushed between.
    "O father, what intends thy hand", she cried,
"Against thy only son? What fury, O son,
Possesses thee to bend that mortal dart
Against thy father's head? and know'st for whom; 730
For him who sits above, and laughs the while
At thee ordained his drudge, to execute
Whate'er his wrath, which he calls justice, bids,
His wrath, which one day will destroy ye both."
    She spake, and at her words the hellish pest 735
Forbore; then these to her Satan returned:
    "So strange thy outcry, and thy words so strange
Thou interposest, that my sudden hand,
Prevented, spares to tell thee yet by deeds
What it intends, till first I know of thee 740
What thing thou art, thus double-formed, and why,
In this infernal vale first met, thou call'st
Me father, and that phantasm call'st my son.
I know thee not, nor ever saw till now
Sight more detestable than him and thee." 745
    To whom thus the portress of Hell-gate replied:
"Hast thou forgot me then, and do I seem
Now in thine eye so foul? once deemed so fair
In Heaven, when at the assembly, and in sight
Of all the Seraphim with thee combined 750

In bold conspiracy against Heaven's King,
All on a sudden miserable pain
Surprised thee; dim thine eyes, and dizzy swum
In darkness, while thy head flames thick and fast
Threw forth, till on the left side opening wide,   755
Likest to thee in shape and countenance bright,
Then shining Heavenly-fair, a goddess armed,
Out of thy head I sprung. Amazement seized
All the host of Heaven; back they recoiled afraid
At first, and called me *Sin*, and for a sign   760
Portentous held me; but, familiar grown,
I pleased, and with attractive graces won
The most averse, thee chiefly, who full oft
Thyself in me thy perfect image viewing
Becam'st enamoured; and such joy thou took'st   765
With me in secret, that my womb conceived
A growing burden. Meanwhile war arose,
And fields were fought in Heaven; wherein remained
(For what could else?) to our almighty foe
Clear victory, to our part loss and rout   770
Through all the Empyrean. Down they fell,
Driven headlong from the pitch of Heaven, down
Into this deep, and in the general fall
I also; at which time this powerful key
Into my hands was given, with charge to keep   775
These gates for ever shut, which none can pass
Without my opening. Pensive here I sat
Alone; but long I sat not, till my womb,
Pregnant by thee, and now excessive grown,
Prodigious motion felt and rueful throes.   780
At last this odious offspring whom thou seest,
Thine own begotten, breaking violent way,

Tore through my entrails, that, with fear and pain
Distorted, all my nether shape thus grew
Transformed; but he, my inbred enemy, 785
Forth issued, brandishing his fatal dart,
Made to destroy. I fled, and cried out *Death!*
Hell trembled at the hideous name, and sighed
From all her caves, and back resounded *Death!*
I fled; but he pursued (though more, it seems, 790
Inflamed with lust than rage) and, swifter far,
Me overtook, his mother, all dismayed,
And, in embraces forcible and foul
Engendering with me, of that rape begot
These yelling monsters, that with ceaseless cry 795
Surround me, as thou saw'st, hourly conceived
And hourly born, with sorrow infinite
To me; for, when they list, into the womb
That bred them they return, and howl, and gnaw
My bowels, their repast; then, bursting forth 800
Afresh, with conscious terrors vex me round,
That rest or intermission none I find.
Before mine eyes in opposition sits
Grim Death, my son and foe, who sets them on,
And me, his parent, would full soon devour 805
For want of other prey, but that he knows
His end with mine involved, and knows that I
Should prove a bitter morsel, and his bane,
Whenever that shall be; so Fate pronounced.
But thou, O father, I forewarn thee, shun 810
His deadly arrow; neither vainly hope
To be invulnerable in those bright arms,
Though tempered heavenly; for that mortal dint,
Save he who reigns above, none can resist."

She finished; and the subtle Fiend his lore   815
Soon learned, now milder, and thus answered smooth:
  "Dear daughter—since thou claim'st me for thy
          sire,
And my fair son here show'st me, the dear pledge
Of dalliance had with thee in Heaven, and joys
Then sweet, now sad to mention, through dire
          change   820
Befallen us unforeseen, unthought of—know
I come no enemy, but to set free
From out this dark and dismal house of pain
Both him and thee, and all the Heavenly host
Of spirits that in our just pretences armed   825
Fell with us from on high. From them I go
This uncouth errand sole, and one for all
Myself expose, with lonely steps to tread
The unfounded deep, and through the void immense
To search with wandering quest a place foretold   830
Should be, and, by concurring signs, ere now
Created vast and round, a place of bliss
In the purlieus of Heaven, and therein placed
A race of upstart creatures, to supply
Perhaps our vacant room, though more removed,   835
Lest Heaven, surcharged with potent multitude,
Might hap to move new broils. Be this or aught
Than this more secret now designed, I haste
To know; and, this once known, shall soon return,
And bring ye to the place where thou and Death   840
Shall dwell at ease, and up and down unseen
Wing silently the buxom air, embalmed
With odours: there ye shall be fed and filled
Immeasurably; all things shall be your prey."

He ceased, for both seemed highly pleased, and
    Death   845
Grinned horrible a ghastly smile, to hear
His famine should be filled, and blessed his maw
Destined to that good hour: no less rejoiced
His mother bad, and thus bespake her sire:
    "The key of this infernal pit, by due   850
And by command of Heaven's all-powerful King,
I keep, by him forbidden to unlock
These adamantine gates; against all force
Death ready stands to interpose his dart,
Fearless to be o'ermatched by living might.   855
But what owe I to his commands above,
Who hates me, and hath hither thrust me down
Into this gloom of Tartarus profound,
To sit in hateful office here confined,
Inhabitant of Heaven and heavenly-born,   860
Here in perpetual agony and pain,
With terrors and with clamours compassed round
Of mine own brood, that on my bowels feed?
Thou art my father, thou my author, thou
My being gav'st me; whom should I obey   865
But thee, whom follow? thou wilt bring me soon
To that new world of light and bliss, among
The gods who live at ease, where I shall reign
At thy right hand voluptuous, as beseems
Thy daughter and thy darling, without end."   870
    Thus saying, from her side the fatal key,
Sad instrument of all our woe, she took;
And, towards the gate rolling her bestial train,
Forthwith the huge portcullis high up-drew,
Which but herself not all the Stygian powers   875

Could once have moved; then in the key-hole turns
The intricate wards, and every bolt and bar
Of massy iron or solid rock with ease
Unfastens: on a sudden open fly
With impetuous recoil and jarring sound   880
The infernal doors, and on their hinges grate
Harsh thunder, that the lowest bottom shook
Of Erebus. She opened, but to shut
Excelled her power; the gates wide open stood,
That with extended wings a bannered host,   885
Under spread ensigns marching, might pass through
With horse and chariots ranked in loose array;
So wide they stood, and like a furnace-mouth
Cast forth redounding smoke and ruddy flame.
Before their eyes in sudden view appear   890
The secrets of the hoary deep, a dark
Illimitable ocean, without bound,
Without dimension; where length, breadth, and
    highth,
And time, and place, are lost; where eldest Night
And Chaos, ancestors of Nature, hold   895
Eternal anarchy, amidst the noise
Of endless wars, and by confusion stand.
For hot, cold, moist, and dry, four champions fierce,
Strive here for mastery, and to battle bring
Their embryon atoms; they around the flag   900
Of each his faction, in their several clans,
Light-armed or heavy, sharp, smooth, swift, or slow,
Swam populous, unnumbered as the sands
Of Barca or Cyrene's torrid soil,
Levied to side with warring winds, and poise   905
Their lighter wings. To whom these most adhere

He rules a moment; Chaos umpire sits,
And by decision more embroils the fray
By which he reigns; next him, high arbiter,
Chance governs all. Into this wild Abyss,   910
The womb of Nature, and perhaps her grave,
Of neither sea, nor shore, nor air, nor fire,
But all these in their pregnant causes mixed
Confusedly, and which thus must ever fight,
Unless the Almighty Maker them ordain   915
His dark materials to create more worlds—
Into this wild Abyss the wary Fiend
Stood on the brink of Hell and looked a while,
Pondering his voyage; for no narrow frith
He had to cross. Nor was his ear less pealed   920
With noises loud and ruinous (to compare
Great things with small) than when Bellona storms,
With all her battering engines bent to rase
Some capital city; or less than if this frame
Of heaven were falling, and these elements   925
In mutiny had from her axle torn
The steadfast Earth. At last his sail-broad vans
He spreads for flight, and in the surging smoke
Uplifted spurns the ground; thence many a league,
As in a cloudy chair, ascending rides   930
Audacious; but, that seat soon failing, meets
A vast vacuity: all unawares,
Fluttering his pennons vain, plumb-down he drops
Ten thousand fadom deep, and to this hour
Down had been falling, had not by ill chance
The strong rebuff of some tumultuous cloud   935
Instinct with fire and nitre, hurried him
As many miles aloft; that fury stayed,

Quenched in a boggy Syrtis, neither sea,
Nor good dry land, nigh foundered, on he fares, 940
Treading the crude consistence, half on foot,
Half flying; behoves him now both oar and sail.
As when a gryphon through the wilderness
With winged course, o'er hill or moory dale,
Pursues the Arimaspian, who by stealth 945
Had from his wakeful custody purloined
The guarded gold: so eagerly the Fiend
O'er bog or steep, through strait, rough, dense, or
          rare,
With head, hands, wings, or feet, pursues his way,
And swims, or sinks, or wades, or creeps, or flies. 950
At length a universal hubbub wild
Of stunning sounds and voices all confused,
Borne through the hollow dark, assaults his ear
With loudest vehemence. Thither he plies
Undaunted to meet there whatever Power 955
Or spirit of the nethermost Abyss
Might in that noise reside, of whom to ask
Which way the nearest coast of darkness lies
Bordering on light; when straight behold the throne
Of Chaos, and his dark pavilion spread 960
Wide on the wasteful Deep. With him enthroned
Sat sable-vested Night, eldest of things,
The consort of his reign; and by them stood
Orcus and Ades, and the dreaded name
Of Demogorgon; Rumour next and Chance, 965
And Tumult and Confusion all embroiled,
And Discord with a thousand various mouths.
    To whom Satan, turning boldly, thus: "Ye Powers
And spirits of this nethermost Abyss,

Chaos and ancient Night, I come no spy,   970
With purpose to explore or to disturb
The secrets of your realm; but, by constraint
Wandering this darksome desert, as my way
Lies through your spacious empire up to light,
Alone and without guide, half lost, I seek   975
What readiest path leads where your gloomy bounds
Confine with Heaven; or if some other place,
From your dominion won, the ethereal King
Possesses lately, thither to arrive
I travel this profound. Direct my course: 980
Directed, no mean recompense it brings
To your behoof, if I that region lost,
All usurpation thence expelled, reduce
To her original darkness and your sway
(Which is my present journey) and once more   985
Erect the standard there of ancient Night.
Yours be the advantage all, mine the revenge."
    Thus Satan; and him thus the Anarch old,
With faltering speech and visage incomposed,
Answered: "I know thee, stranger, who thou art, 990
That mighty leading angel, who of late
Made head against Heaven's King, though over-
    thrown.
I saw and heard; for such a numerous host
Fled not in silence through the frighted deep,
With ruin upon ruin, rout on rout,   995
Confusion worse confounded; and Heaven-gates
Poured out by millions her victorious bands,
Pursuing. I upon my frontiers here
Keep residence; if all I can will serve
That little which is left so to defend,   1000

Encroached on still through our intestine broils
Weakening the sceptre of old Night: first Hell,
Your dungeon, stretching far and wide beneath;
Now lately heaven and earth, another world
Hung o'er my realm, linked in a golden chain 1005
To that side Heaven from whence your legions fell.
If that way be your walk, you have not far;
So much the nearer danger. Go, and speed;
Havoc and spoil and ruin are my gain."
  He ceased; and Satan stayed not to reply, 1010
But, glad that now his sea should find a shore,
With fresh alacrity and force renewed
Springs upward, like a pyramid of fire,
Into the wild expanse, and through the shock
Of fighting elements, on all sides round 1015
Environed, wins his way; harder beset
And more endangered, than when Argo passed
Through Bosporus betwixt the justling rocks;
Or when Ulysses on the larboard shunned
Charybdis, and by the other whirlpool steered: 1020
So he with difficulty and labour hard
Moved on; with difficulty and labour he.
But, he once passed, soon after, when Man fell,
Strange alteration! Sin and Death amain
Following his track (such was the will of
    Heaven) 1025
Paved after him a broad and beaten way
Over the dark Abyss, whose boiling gulf
Tamely endured a bridge of wondrous length,
From Hell continued, reaching the utmost orb
Of this frail world; by which the spirits perverse 1030
With easy intercourse pass to and fro

To tempt or punish mortals, except whom
God and good angels guard by special grace.
    But now at last the sacred influence
Of light appears, and from the walls of Heaven   1035
Shoots far into the bosom of dim Night
A glimmering dawn. Here Nature first begins
Her fardest verge, and Chaos to retire,
As from her outmost works, a broken foe,
With tumult less and with less hostile din;   1040
That Satan with less toil, and now with ease,
Wafts on the calmer wave by dubious light,
And like a weather-beaten vessel holds
Gladly the port, though shrouds and tackle torn;
Or in the emptier waste, resembling air,   1045
Weighs his spread wings, at leisure to behold
Far off the empyreal Heaven, extended wide
In circuit, undetermined square or round,
With opal towers and battlements adorned
Of living sapphire, once his native seat;   1050
And fast by, hanging in a golden chain,
This pendent world, in bigness as a star
Of smallest magnitude close by the moon.
Thither, full fraught with mischievous revenge,
Accurst, and in a cursed hour, he hies.   1055

NOTES

Book I

1. *Of Man's first disobedience.* In his very first words Milton announces the subject of the whole work, as the great classical poets had done. Lines 1–26 form an introduction to the whole of *Paradise Lost*, lines 27–49 to the first book.

2. *mortal* here means 'causing death' (as in 'mortal wound'). The fruit of the forbidden tree was 'mortal' because God had declared that "in the day that thou eatest thereof thou shalt surely die." (Genesis, ii, 17.)

4. *Eden* is, strictly speaking, the whole land of which Paradise is a part; but here (and elsewhere) the word means 'Paradise.' (Eden itself was not lost, for in the last line of the last book we read that Adam and Eve, exiled from Paradise, "through Eden took their solitary way.")

4. *one greater Man:* Christ, the Messiah.
So I Corinthians xxi, 22: "Since by man came death, by man came also the resurrection of the dead. For as in Adam all die, even so in Christ shall all be made alive"; Romans v, 19: "For as by one man's disobedience many were made sinners, so by the obedience of one shall many be made righteous."

5. *Restore.* In the subjunctive because the restoration is not yet fully accomplished.

6. *heavenly Muse.* The Muses were goddesses who inspired men with love of the arts, and whose aid the classical poets very often invoked at the beginning of their

works. So too Milton asks the help of the "heavenly Muse" at the beginning of the *Nativity Ode* (15).

His "heavenly Muse," however, though the same in name, is not quite the same as the classical Muse, and in the present instance seems to be the Holy Spirit, by whom Moses, David, and the prophets were inspired. Milton very often makes use of both the classical and the biblical tradition in this way; though it seems surprising to us, both were so familiar in his day that it did not then seem incongruous.

6. *secret* probably means 'set apart.' *Cf. Nativity Ode*, 28, "from out his secret altar." When God gave his commandments to Moses on Mount Sinai the people were strictly forbidden to ascend the mountain (Exodus xix, 12).

7. *Oreb* (Horeb). Horeb and Sinai are probably alternative names for the same mountain; in Exodus xix, 11 it is called Sinai, but in Deuteronomy iv, 10, Horeb. Or they may indicate two peaks of one mountain.

8. *That shepherd:* Moses. He was a shepherd literally for he kept the flock of Jethro (Exodus iii, 1) and also figuratively, as leader of the Israelites (Psalm 77, 20: "Thou leddest thy people like a flock by the hand of Moses and Aaron").

8. *first taught*. In Genesis i.

10. *Rose*. Notice the effect of the strong accent on the first syllable of the line, and of the use of a monosyllable in this emphatic way. The result is to give a vivid idea of 'rising.'

10. *Chaos*. Again a classical idea adapted to the biblical tradition. In Greek mythology Chaos was the formless matter out of which the world was made.

10. *Sion* (=Zion) and Moriah are the hills on which Jerusalem was built. The Temple was on Moriah, while Zion was called "the city of David."

11. *Siloa* (= Siloam) is usually called a pool, but its waters overflowed and formed a rivulet which watered the 'King's Garden.'

12. *the oracle of God:* the Temple. Solomon's temple is called "the oracle" in I Kings vi, 19–20.

Milton suggests a parallel between the pool of Siloa, close to the Temple, and the spring near the altar of Zeus on Mount Helicon, the favourite haunt of the Muses.

15. *Aonian Mount:* Helicon in Boeotia. Aonia is an old name for the district. Milton means that his poem is to surpass the great poems of Greece and Rome because it is about a greater subject and is inspired by the Holy Spirit, not by the Muses.

15. *pursues,* 'treats of.'

16. *Things unattempted.* This is a claim frequently made by poets of every age, and by the Attendant Spirit in Milton's *Comus* (43).

> . . . for I will tell you now
> What never yet was heard in tale or song.

16. *rhyme* here means 'verse'—there are of course no rhymes in *Paradise Lost.* So in *Lycidas* (10), ". . . he knew/Himself to sing and build the lofty rhyme."

18. *Before all temples, cf.* I Corinthians iii, 16. "Know ye not that ye are the temple of God, and that the Spirit of God dwelleth in you?"

19–22. The Spirit now invoked by Milton is the Spirit of God, which at the Creation "moved upon the face of the waters" (Genesis i, 2).

With this passage compare VII, 234:

> . . . on the watery calm
> His brooding wings the Spirit of God outspread,
> And vital virtue infused, and vital warmth
> Throughout the fluid mass.

The word "brooding" which Milton uses in both places is probably the real meaning of the Hebrew word translated "moved" in the Authorized Version. Milton knew Hebrew and could read the Old Testament in the original language.

21. *Dove-like*, because the Spirit of God appeared in the form of a dove at the baptism of Jesus (St Matthew iii, 16; St Luke iii, 22).

21. *Abyss:* the Chaos of line 10. The original meaning of the Greek word is 'gap' or 'void.'

24. *highth*. Milton always uses this form of the word.

24. *argument*, 'subject.' The summaries at the beginning of each book of *Paradise Lost* are called "arguments."

25. *assert*, 'vindicate.'

26. *justify*, 'prove just.' Probably the sense is "justify to men," as in *Samson Agonistes* (293–294) "Just are the ways of God/And justifiable to men."

29. *grand*, 'first,' *cf.* 'grandfather,' or possibly 'great,' *cf.* 122, "our grand foe."

32. *For one restraint*, 'an account of one restriction, though they were lords of the world otherwise.' Or possibly (with a comma after "will"), 'though they were lords of all the rest of the world, but for one restriction.' It is even possible that as we read we should be aware of both senses at once.

34. *serpent:* Satan, who later took the form of a serpent to deceive Eve.

35. *envy*, first of the honour bestowed upon the Son (V, 662 *ff.*) and after Satan's fall, of Adam and Eve (IV, 358 *ff.*).

35. *revenge, i.e.,* desire for revenge on God, by frustrating his intentions.

38. This line ends with an extra, unemphatic syllable, a rare thing in Milton.

39. *in glory*, i.e., the glory belonging only to God and the Son, as line 40 makes clear.

This is the crime of which God accuses him (V, 725): "who intends to erect his throne/Equal to ours." "Above his peers" merely explains "glory" and is not the real crime.

39. *peers*, 'equals.' This meaning is still found in 'peerless' = 'without equal.'

45–49. These lines have many echoes of scripture, *e.g.*, Isaiah xiv, 12, "How art thou fallen from heaven, O Lucifer, son of the morning!" St Luke x, 18, "I beheld Satan as lightning fall from heaven." Jude 6, "and the angels which kept not their first estate, he hath reserved in everlasting chains under darkness."

45. *the ethereal sky:* the abode of God. In Homer the 'ether' was a realm of pure and quiet air above the denser atmosphere of the earth, and was the home of the gods.

46. *ruin* in its Latin sense of 'crashing downfall,' takes up "headlong" of line 45, and "combustion" similarly takes up "flaming."

46. *down*. Notice how this emphatic short word coming after the longer ones in the first part of this line gives the idea of the sudden violent fall.

48. *adamantine chains*. 'Adamant' was the name of a metal which was supposed to be unbreakable; the word is the same as 'diamonds.' The phrase "adamantine chains" is a favourite of poets from Aeschylus onward.

50 *ff*. The real action of the story now begins, the introduction and the description of Satan being ended.

55. *lasting pain*. Before their fall, the angels felt no pain. When Satan is wounded in the fight against the Archangel Michael he "first knew pain." (VI, 327.)

56. *baleful* may mean either 'sorrowful,' or 'bringing sorrow,' 'harmful'; or very likely both at once.

57. *witnessed*, 'bore witness to,' 'showed.' The word is

always used in this sense by Milton, not in the weaker sense of 'saw.' The "affliction" and "dismay" are of course Satan's—he was not merely observing some one else's misery, but showing his own.

58. *obdurate*. The accent is on the second syllable, as always in Milton.

59. *as far as angels ken*, 'as far as angels see.' Some people think that "ken" is a noun, and "angels" a genitive ("angel's") giving the meaning 'as far as an angel's sight.' But the first seems the simpler explanation.

60. *situation*, 'place.'

60–64. Satan uses words very like these when answering Beelzebub in lines 180–183.

63. *darkness visible*. Absolute darkness is invisible, but "visible darkness" is just so dark that one can see a little.

In *Il Penseroso* (79–80) Milton says, "where glowing embers through the room/Teach light to counterfeit a gloom."—a very similar idea, the embers producing the effect which the "great furnace" produces here. In lines 181–183 Satan again refers to these lightless flames. It was a common belief that the flames of Hell gave no light, since all was dark in Hell.

64. *discover*, 'uncover,' or 'disclose.'

66. *hope never comes*. These words recall the inscription over the gates of Hell in Dante (*Inferno* III, 9), "All hope abandon, ye who enter here." Milton knew and greatly admired Dante's work.

68. *Still*, 'constantly.' *Cf.* Shakespeare, *The Tempest* I, ii, 229, "the still-vexed Bermoothes," where "still-vexed" means 'continually tormented by storms.'

69. *urges*, 'oppresses,' the Latin meaning.

71. *those rebellious*. We still use adjectives for nouns in this way, but only with the article; "the rebellious" would not seem strange.

72. *utter*, 'outer,' not 'complete.'

Cf. *Paradise Lost* III, 16, "Through utter and through middle darkness borne." The idea is that in St Matthew viii, 12, "the children of the Kingdom shall be cast out into outer darkness."

74. *centre* probably means 'the earth,' which was the centre of the universe according to the Ptolemaic theory. *Cf.* 686, "ransacked the centre."

74. *utmost pole*: the pole of the universe, not that of the earth. The earth was believed to be the centre of a series of 'spheres,' one pole of which pointed to the 'ethereal heaven' far beyond, the other being at the lowest point of Hell. (See Introduction, p. 29.) Milton borrows this measurement of the distance between Hell and Heaven from Homer and Virgil and seems to have been interested in the idea, as he uses it again in *Doctrine and Discipline of Divorce*, II, 3, when he refers to "that uttermost and bottomless gulf of Chaos, deeper from holy bliss than the world's diameter multiplied."

75. The sudden mention of Heaven is unexpected and makes the horrors of Hell the more vivid by contrast.

80. *Palestine:* Philistia.

81. *Beelzebub:* a god of the Philistines. In St Matthew xii, 24 he is called "the prince of the devils," so that he might well rank next to Satan. In V, 671 *ff.* he is called Satan's "next subordinate," and addressed as "companion dear" by him.

82. *thence.* The word 'Satan' means 'enemy.'

84–124. Satan's speech is difficult to follow, for he is angry and incoherent—for instance the two sentences beginning with "if" (84 and 87) are never completed—but his undaunted spirit and determination to continue the struggle are clear.

84. Milton here recalls Isaiah xiv, 12, "How art thou fallen from heaven, O Lucifer, Son of the Morning" (this

refers, however, to the King of Babylon, not to Satan), and Virgil, *Aeneid* II, 274, "quantum mutatus ab illo/Hectore." ('How changed from that great Hector.')

86. *didst* should in strict grammar be 'did,' since the antecedent of "who" is "him." But we readily understand 'thou.'

87. *if he. I.e.*, 'If thou beest he.'

90. 'Whom' should be understood before "now," carrying on "whom" in 87.

93. *He:* God, whom Satan will not name. So also line 257, "all but less than he/Whom thunder hath made greater."

93. *till then, i.e.*, till the battle between God and the rebel angels, described in Book VI.

94. *for*, 'because of.'

95–97. Some editors think that this is borrowed from Prometheus' taunt to Zeus in Aeschylus' *Prometheus Bound*, 992–997. Milton no doubt knew the passage and may have had it in mind, but if he had not himself endowed Satan with these characteristics, there would have been no such poem as *Paradise Lost*.

97. *fixed*, 'steadfast.' *Cf. Il Penseroso*, 4, "Or fill the fixed mind with all your toys."

98. *from*, 'arising from.'

98. *injured merit.* Satan is always pre-eminent among the angels. So in II, 5,

> Satan exalted sat, by merit raised
> To that bad eminence.

His "merit" was injured because the Son was honoured above him. "Merit" is used not of course in the sense of 'virtue' but in that of 'deserving'—one may even 'merit' punishment.

101. *Innumerable force*, 'countless army.' Or "innumerable" may really belong to "spirits" in sense.

102. This line has an extra syllable, which helps to stress the word "me," already emphatic.

104. *dubious.* The battle went on for three days, and at its
     end the rebel angels were defeated but, as we now see,
     not utterly. This was however the intention of God,
     cf. VI, 854, "... he meant/Not to destroy, but root them
     out of Heaven."

     Satan exaggerates in calling the battle "dubious," as
     also in saying "shook his throne."

105. *field,* 'battle.'

107. *study,* 'striving after,' the Latin meaning of the word.

109. This is a difficult line. Keeping the question-mark at
     the end of the line as in the older editions, we may para-
     phrase, 'and in what else does invincibility consist?' or
     'and what other quality is invincible [except those just
     mentioned]?'

     Some editors put a semi-colon instead of a question-
     mark; then "what ... else" would mean 'whatever else'
     (or 'whatever other quality') is invincible—completing
     the list of qualities which make up invincibility. The first
     meaning is the more likely. If it is right it contains a
     piece of irony at Satan's expense. He asserts that the
     really invincible things are negative, having to do with
     hatred and resistance. The course of the poem proves
     that the creative instinct of love is the stronger.

110. *That glory* probably means the glory God would
     acquire by having forced Satan to submit. It might
     however mean Satan's own glory as being unconquer-
     able; but this would be difficult to fit in with "extort."

114. *Doubted,* 'feared for.'

114. *empire,* 'power.'

     This statement is another of Satan's exaggerations.

114. *that*—emphatic, carried on by "that were an igno-
     miny," and "This downfall."

115. Through the word "ignominy" Milton inserts an
     extra syllable in this line, but there is no difficulty in the
     reading if you stress the first syllable of the word

strongly. The same thing happens in II, 207, "Exile, or ignominy, or bonds, or pain."

115. *beneath*, 'even lower than.'

116. *since*, followed by "since" in 118. Satan gives two reasons for hope, (1) that the angels are immortal, (2) that they have learned by experience. But, as elsewhere, he is somewhat incoherent; the two clauses do not balance, and the second has no finite verb, but merges into the conclusion.

116. *by fate*, 'in accordance with the decrees of fate,' implying that fate is above God, as it was believed to be above the gods of classical mythology; so in V, 861–862 the angels come into being, not by God's creation but their own, "when fatal course/Had circled his full orb," *i.e.*, when the time decreed by fate had come. But in VII, 172 God declares "necessity and chance/Approach me not, and what I will is fate."

116. *gods:* divine beings.

117. *empyreal*, 'fiery.' The bodies (if they can be called so) of the angels were supposed to be formed from fire, as was to be expected of beings who lived in the 'empyrean,' the heaven which is the sphere of fire. So Milton calls the angels "Ye flaming Powers" and speaks of their "fiery essence," in his poem *Upon the Circumcision*. He would of course have regarded the fire as spiritual, not actual, and used the word "ethereal" as an equivalent. There is scriptural authority for the "fiery essence" of the angels in Psalm 104, 4, "Who maketh his angels spirits; his ministers a flaming fire."

Note that Milton always accents "empýreal," but "empyréan."

Satan is certain of the immortality of the angels, Beelzebub accepts this, but derives no hope from it, only foreseeing unending misery (I, 139–155). Moloch (II, 99–101) and Belial (II, 142 *ff.*) are doubtful.

120. *more successful hope*, 'more hope of success.'

122–123. Each of these lines can be scanned in two different ways:

    (1) Irreconcílable to our grand foe

    (2) Irréconcílable . . .

and

    (1) Who now triúmphs

    (2)   . . .   tríumphs

122. *grand*, 'great.'

124. *tyranny*, "Tyranny and superstition" are twice mentioned together by Milton in his prose works as the worst dangers to man. What Satan here calls "the tyranny of Heaven" Milton himself called "the throne and monarchy of God" (42).

127. *compeer*, like "peer" (39) means 'equal,' here 'companion.'

    Although Beelzebub is called Satan's "bold compeer," he is much more despondent and does not equal him in determination; his speech is practical, and lacks the fierce idealism of Satan's.

128. *throned powers*. Probably "throned" refers to the dignity of the angels before they fell, as in 360 "powers that erst in Heaven sat on thrones," and not to the hierarchies of angels.

129. *Seraphim*. The Hebrew plural of 'Seraph.'

130. *conduct*, 'command.'

131–132. Beelzebub repeats Satan's exaggerated statement in 103–105 and 113–114.

136. *and all this mighty host*. Sc. "I see" (134).

138. *essences*, 'spirits.'

139. *remains*. In the singular, because "mind and spirit" are one idea.

140. *vigour soon returns*. So in VI, 330, when Satan is wounded "the ethereal substance closed,/Not long divisible."

141. *extinct*, 'extinguished.' Supply 'be' here and with "swallowed up" (142).

141. *happy state*. *Sc.* 'our.'

144. *Of force*, 'perforce.' *Cf.* IV, 812–813, "but returns/Of force to its own likeness."

146 *ff.* The immortality of the angels, which gave Satan so much confidence, seems to Beelzebub only an addition to their misery.

148. *suffice*, 'satisfy.'

150. *his business:* the business appointed by God for them to do, as in II, 70, "his own invented torments," *i.e.*, those invented by him for us to endure.

152. *the gloomy deep:* Chaos.

155. *To undergo*, 'for undergoing,' depending on "strength" and "being"; or perhaps 'so as to undergo.'

157. *Cherub*. The Cherubim (Cherubs) were the second highest of the orders of angels. See Introduction, p. 31.

158. *Doing or suffering*. *I.e.*, whether carrying out God's orders (149 *ff.*) or enduring torment (155). In II, 199 Belial uses the same words, "To suffer, as to do/Our strength is equal." There may also be a hint of the Greek proverbial contrast of 'to do' (to be active) and 'to suffer' (to be passive).

160–162. Satan does not delight in doing evil merely for its own sake, but with the deliberate purpose of opposing God.

165. Satan's plan is completely reversed, as we see at the end of the poem (XII, 469–471) where Adam says:

> O goodness infinite, goodness immense,
> That all this good of evil shall produce,
> And evil turn to good.

167. *if I fail not*, 'if I am not mistaken.'

170. *His ministers:* the good angels.

It has been pointed out that in Raphael's account of the battle (VI, 80 *ff.*) the Son alone drives out the rebel angels, having expressly ordered the good angels to stand aside and merely watch. If this inconsistency troubles us, we can explain it by saying that Satan refuses to give the glory of the victory to the Son, just as he refused to name God as the victor (93), and prefers to attribute his defeat to the other angels.

172. *o'erblown*, 'blown over,' 'ceased to blow.'

172. *laid*, 'laid to rest,' 'calmed.' We still speak of 'laying a ghost,' or of a shower 'laying the dust.'

176. *his*, 'its.' 'His' was generally used at this period as the neuter possessive pronoun. (See note on 254.)

178. *slip*, 'let slip.'

178. *occasion*, 'opportunity.'

178–179. 'Whether contempt for us or the satisfaction of his fury has caused our foe to give us this opportunity.'

179. *satiate*, 'satiated.' This short form of the past participle is common in Elizabethan English; it is closer to the Latin than the usual form in -*ed*. *Cf.* "uplift" (193).

181. *seat*, 'home.'

183. *tend*, 'make our way.'

185. *harbour*, 'dwell.'

186. *afflicted*, in the literal sense of the Latin word, 'struck down,' 'shattered.'

186. *powers*, 'forces.'

187. *offend*, 'injure,' another Latin meaning.

190–191. A very short way of saying 'if we may not gain reinforcement from hope, (let us consult) what resolution we may gain from despair.' With each clause from 187 to 191 we must supply "let us" (from 183) and "consult" (from 187).

191. We here come to a definite pause. Satan has made his decision, and Milton marks this by a digression for description and reference to various stories.

193. *uplift*. See note on 179.

195. *large*, 'wide' (as in French).

197. *As whom*, 'like those creatures whom.'

197. *the fables:* classical mythology. Milton uses a contemptuous word, to imply that these stories are untrue.

198. *Titanian.* The Titans were children of Uranus (Heaven) and Ge (Earth); they rebelled against Uranus, and made one of themselves, Saturn, King of the Gods.

198. *Earth-born.* The Giants were the children of Earth and Heaven, and they rebelled against Zeus (Jove) ("that warred on Jove") as the Titans had against Uranus, but were defeated.

199. *Briareos.* ("Briáreos" here, but generally "Bríareus," with three syllables.) He too was a child of Earth and Heaven, but neither a Titan nor a Giant. However he was what we now call a giant, and had a hundred arms.

199. *Typhon* (or Typhoeus) was a monster with a hundred heads who lived in Cilicia (Tarsus was the chief city of Cilicia, for which it stands here).

201. *Leviathan.* Whatever the Leviathan mentioned in the Bible (Job xli, 1, Psalm 104, 26, Isaiah xxvii, 1) may be, it is clear that Milton is thinking of the whale, although whales do not have scales (206). The story of the sailors mooring their boat to a whale has been told many times, as for instance in the story of Sindbad the Sailor and the Voyages of St Brendan. Milton probably knew it from the book of Olaus Magnus, a Swedish historian, which was written in 1555 and translated into English in 1658. (Milton could of course have used the Latin version.) Hence the mention of Norway.

202. Notice the heavy, rather awkward movement of this line, to suggest the bulk of Leviathan.

202. *ocean stream.* The Greeks thought that the earth (regarded of course as flat) was encircled by a river which they called Ocean.

203. This digression about the sailors brings in the thought

of humanity, instead of the supernatural beings with whom we have been concerned.

204. *night-foundered*, 'overwhelmed by night.' The same word occurs also in *Comus* (483), "some one like us night-foundered here."

206. *With fixed anchor*, 'having fixed his anchor,' a Latin construction. "Fixed" of course goes closely with "in his scaly rind."

207. *Moors*, intransitive.

207. *under the lee:* on the sheltered side of the whale.

208. *Invests* means 'clothes as with a garment,' 'covers.'

211. *Had*, 'would have.'

211–220. In these lines Milton sets forth one of the most important ideas of the whole poem, and his scheme of divine justice. Note the clearness and simplicity of the language.

213. *at large*, 'free' (to carry out his designs).

216–218. For this idea *cf.* XII, 469–471, and see note on 165.

226. *incumbent*, 'resting on.'

230. *And such appeared*. Understand after "and" the relative 'that,' with "land" as its antecedent.

230–237. This simile is difficult to follow because it depends on a theory of volcanic eruptions and on a technical term of alchemy which are strange to us. Volcanic eruptions are supposed to be originated by underground winds; these are reinforced by minerals, such as sulphur, which have caught fire and so been vaporized, in which form they "aid the winds." The floor of the volcano is thus left bare, burnt, and giving out evil smells and smoke.

The point of the comparison comes at the very end—"and such appeared in hue" (230) is taken up by "such resting found the sole/Of unblest feet" (237–238). The dry land of Hell is like the smoking ground which is left exposed after the eruption of a volcano.

232. *Pelorus:* the cape at the N.E. corner of Sicily, not far from Mount Etna. It is now called Cape Faro.

234. *fuelled,* either 'acting as fuel,' or 'filled with fuel.'

234. *conceiving.* We say 'catching' fire, for which 'conceiving' is the Latin expression.

235. *Sublimed.* To 'sublime' or 'sublimate' was a term used in chemistry to mean purifying by fire and converting into vapour.

235. *mineral fury:* the violence of the burning minerals.

236. *involved,* 'wrapped.'

238. *next mate:* Beelzebub.

239. *Stygian flood.* Styx was one of the rivers of Hades (Hell) in Greek mythology. The name comes to be used for ades or Hell in general, and the adjective 'Stygian' in the same sense (*cf.* II, 506, "The Stygian council"). "The Stygian flood" is of course the "burning lake" (210).

240. They appear to themselves to be gods, because they think they have escaped by their own efforts and not by the consent of God; whereas the opposite was the truth (210–213.)

242. *clime,* 'place.' *Cf.* II, 572, ". . . if any clime perhaps/ Might yield them easier habitation."

244. *change,* 'take in exchange.'

246. *sovran.* This form of the word is derived from the Italian, and is in fact more correct than our spelling 'sovereign.'

246. *dispose,* 'do as he wishes.'

247. *fardest,* a variant of 'farthest,' preferred by Milton.

248. *reason, i.e.,* 'our reason.' Satan claims that the fallen angels are the equals of God in intelligence, though inferior in power.

254–255. One of the 'familiar quotations' to be derived from Milton. The idea was a favourite one of the Stoics, and is found in Horace (*Epist.* I, xi, 27). In Milton's time

it was well known and we find echoes of it in many
writers, *e.g.*, Shakespeare, *Hamlet* II, ii, 250, "for there
is nothing either good or bad but t hinking makes it so."
For the rather narrower version of it, that Hell is not a
place but a state of mind, *cf.* IV, 20:

> . . . for within him Hell
> He brings, and round about him, nor from Hell
> One step no more than from himself can fly
> By change of place.

and Marlowe, *Doctor Faustus*, II, i, 122–124:

> Hell hath no limits, nor is circumscribed
> In one self place; but where we are is Hell,
> And where Hell is, there must we ever be.

In the end Satan is not able to live up to his boast, but
so far from being able to "make a Heaven of Hell," he
cries, "Which way I fly is Hell; myself am Hell." (IV,
75.)

254. *its.* Strange as it seems to us, the word 'its' did not
exist in the language till the end of the sixteenth century
and did not come into general use till the middle of the
seventeenth century. (It does not occur at all in the
Authorized Version of the Bible, 1611.) 'His' and occa-
sionally 'her' were the usual forms, together with 'of it,'
'thereof,' etc. Milton uses 'its' only three times in the
whole of his poetry—here, in IV, 813, and in the *Nativity Ode*, 106. 'His' and 'her' occur frequently where we
should use 'its,' in general merely as the possessive of
'it,' but sometimes because the thing to which it refers
is personified. You will easily find instances as you read
the poem.

257. *all but less than he.* No satisfactory explanation has yet
been given of this difficult phrase. It appears to be a
combination of two phrases—(1) 'all but equal to,' (2)
'only less than.' But it does not seem like Milton to
make such a confusion.

260. *for his envy*. God has not made Hell so attractive that he would envy Satan the possession of it.

261. *secure* may mean either 'safe,' or 'free from care.'

263. In VI, 183 Abdiel, the faithful angel, says to Satan:

> Reign thou in Hell thy Kingdom; let me serve
> In Heaven God ever blest . . .
> Yet chains in Hell, not realms expect.

266. *astonished* means 'struck by thunder,' here literally, 'stunned.'

266. *oblivious*, 'causing oblivion.' *Cf.* II, 74, "that forgetful lake."

268. *mansion*, 'dwelling-place,' the original Latin meaning. *Cf.* St John xiv, 2, "In my Father's house are many mansions."

276. *edge*, 'front line.'

281. *astounded*. See note on *astonished* (266).

281. *amazed* had a much stronger meaning in Milton's times than it has now, just as "astounded" and "astonished" had.

282. *pernicious*, 'destructive,' or even 'death-dealing,' the basic meaning of the word.

283. *superior*, 'higher' in rank.

284. *Was moving*, 'began to move,' one of the meanings of the Latin imperfect tense.

Satan began to retrace his steps to the burning lake to summon the other fallen angels.

285. *temper*. To temper metal is to give it the desired quality of hardness etc. by the proper mixture of its ingredients. This quality is 'temper'; but here "temper" means the thing tempered, *i.e.*, the shield. *Cf.* IV, 810:

> Him thus intent Ithuriel with his spear
> Touched lightly; for no falsehood can endure
> Touch of celestial temper.

288. *optic glass*, the usual word for a telescope.

288. *the Tuscan artist:* Galileo. Though he did not actually

invent the telescope, Galileo greatly improved it, and was the first to use it for the study of astronomy, so discovering the rings of Saturn and the satellites of Jupiter. Milton greatly admired Galileo, and when in Florence in 1638 actually visited him at his home not far from the city. He refers to him by name in V, 261:

> . . . as when by night the glass
> Of Galileo, less assured, observes
> Imagined lands and regions in the moon.

289. *Fesole*, now called Fiesole, lies on a hill near Florence.

290. *Valdarno:* (Val d'Arno) 'the Valley of the Arno' (the river which flows through Florence).

292. *to equal which,* 'compared with which.'

293. *Hewn on Norwegian hills.* Norway furnished large quantities of pine-trees for the masts of the ships of all nations, as well as wood for their hulls.

294. *ammiral,* (= admiral) a word of Arabic origin, meaning (1) the commander of a fleet, (2) the flag-ship, or any great ship, as here. Milton deliberately uses the form "ammiral," evidently preferring its sound to "admiral."

296. *marl* literally means 'chalky soil,' but here 'soil' or 'earth' in general.

297. *Heaven's azure.* The blue sky serves as the floor of heaven.

298. *Vaulted.* The fire was all round and above him.

299. *Nathless,* an old form of 'nevertheless.'

300. *inflamed,* 'burning.'

301. *entranced,* 'in a trance.'

302. *Thick as autumnal leaves.* This comparison has been used by many poets—Homer, Virgil, Dante, etc.—but Milton makes it much more vivid by the further description ("that strow the brooks") and by the particular mention of Vallombrosa.

302. *strow,* 'strew.'

303. *Vallombrosa:* ('the shady valley') a famous beauty-

spot near Florence, where there was a monastery. Milton visited it in the autumn of 1638. Note how this part of the poem (288–304) is made more real and lively by Milton's vivid recollection of his stay in Florence, of which he writes in several other places with keen delight.

303. *Etrurian*, *i.e.*, Tuscan—Etruria being the old name of Tuscany.

304. *embower*, 'form bowers.'

304. *or scattered sedge*, *sc.* 'thick as.' Sedge here means sea-weed, not a river-weed as usually. There is said to be a great deal of floating sea-weed in the Red Sea, so that its Hebrew name was the Sea of Sedge.

305. *Orion:* A famous hunter in Greek mythology. After his death he was turned into a constellation, which has the form of a giant equipped ("armed") with a sword, a club, a lion's skin, and a belt. At the times of the rising and setting of the constellation of Orion (at midsummer and in November) bad weather was supposed to prevail.

306. *vexed*, 'troubled,' 'harassed' (the Latin meaning of the word).

306–311. See Exodus xiv.

307. *Busiris*. Milton wishes to make the story more realistic by giving a personal name to the ruler called Pharaoh in the Bible, that being only a title. He chooses the name of Busiris, a legendary King of Egypt said to have been killed by Heracles, and certainly not the Pharaoh of the Bible.

307. *Memphian*. Memphis was the ancient capital of Egypt, near which are the Pyramids. Here "Memphian" means 'Egyptian.' *Cf.* "Memphian Kings" (694).

307. *chivalry* is usually associated with medieval knights, or at least with cavalry (from which the word is derived). But it can also mean any forces or army, as here. *Cf. Paradise Regained* III, 344, "Such and so numerous was

their chivalry," where "chivalry" = 'forces,' as just before (338).

308. *perfidious* because Pharaoh had first given the Israelites permission to depart and then pursued them.

309. *Goshen:* the country on the eastern side of the Nile, where the Israelites under Joseph originally settled. (Genesis xlvii) and where their descendants lived for 430 years (Exodus xii, 40).

The story of the overwhelming of the Egyptians is introduced by the mention of the "scattered sedge" of the Red Sea, to which the multitude of the fallen angels is compared; it ends by suggesting a comparison of the drowned Egyptians with the same angels, so forming a complete circle, as it were.

312. *Abject,* 'thrown down'—the Latin meaning.

312. *these:* the fallen angels.

313. *Under amazement of,* 'utterly bewildered by.'

315–330. This speech of Satan's is somewhat incoherent, though less so than his first. He speaks to the other angels in a different tone from that which he used in speaking to Beelzebub, taunting and scolding them instead of arguing. At the end he drops his ironical tone, and after warning them of the fate in store for them unless they rouse themselves, he pauses and suddenly shouts the challenging call to action "Awake, arise, or be for ever fallen!"

316–317. Heaven is lost to them if they can be so stupefied.

318. *or,* anticipating the second "or" in 322.

320. *virtue,* 'valour.'

320. *for,* 'because of.'

320. *ease,* 'relaxation,' 'comfort.' *Cf.* 'to take one's ease.'

321. *To slumber,* 'in slumbering.'

325. *ensigns,* 'standards.'

332. *wont,* 'are wont.' *Cf.* "Where champions bold/Wont ride." (764.)

335. *Nor did they not* = 'they did.' The double negative is an emphatic way of stating what would normally be put in an affirmative way. It is a Latin device.

337. *to . . . obeyed.* The verb 'to obey' takes the dative case in Latin, French, etc.

338. *Innumerable.* Notice how emphatic this word is because of its position at the beginning of the line and the pause which follows it. It is followed by two similes, adding to its impressiveness—the fallen angels are compared for their numbers first, when flying, to the locusts which descended upon Egypt (338–343); then, after landing on the plain, to the hordes of barbarians which overran the Roman Empire (351–355). They have already been compared, when lying on the fiery lake, to the fallen autumn leaves (302–303). Each simile suits the particular situation of the angels.

338–343. The account of the plague of locusts is given in Exodus x, 12–15; Milton keeps very closely to the scriptural account, sometimes using the same words.

339. *Amram's son:* Moses. (Exodus vi, 20.)

339. *Egypt's evil day* refers to the plagues called down upon Egypt by Moses (Exodus vii–xii).

340. *coast,* 'region,' 'country.'

340. *pitchy,* as we say 'pitch-dark.'

341. *warping* is really a technical term in seamanship, but Milton here uses it to indicate an irregular forward movement.

345. *cope.* A cope is (1) a long cloak or cape, (2) a covering, (3) a canopy or vault like that of the sky. There was a phrase 'under the cope of heaven' meaning 'under heaven' or 'in all the world,' in very frequent use from the fourteenth century onward. Milton probably has this in mind, adapting it to suit the context.

347–348. *the uplifted spear . . . waving,* 'as the spear was uplifted and waved,'—an 'absolute' construction as in Latin.

350. *brimstone:* sulphur, as is suggested by the comparison to the floor of a volcano in 236–237.

351. *multitude.* The Goths, Huns, and Vandals, who over-ran Southern Europe and sacked Athens and Rome (A.D. 410). The Vandals went to Spain and crossed the Straits of Gibraltar, finally settling in North Africa. This passage shows the interest in history which Milton is known to have had.

353. *Rhene or the Danaw.* "Rhene" is the Latin form of 'Rhine,' 'Donau' ("Danaw") the German name for the Danube. These forms were usual in Milton's time. The Rhine and the Danube formed the boundaries of the Roman empire.

355. *Beneath,* 'south of.'

355. *Libyan sands:* the northern coast of Africa.

361 *ff.* The names of the rebel angels were utterly forgotten after their fall, as Milton tells us again in VI, 378–380:

> . . . yet by doom
> Cancelled from Heaven and sacred memory,
> Nameless in dark oblivion let them dwell.

It was the general belief in the Middle Ages and later that the pagan gods were really the fallen angels and the devils of scripture. It is therefore by the names of these pagan gods that they must now be called, since they have no others.

362. *blotted out . . . from the Books of Life.* Cf. Revelation iii, 5, "I will not blot out his name out of the book of life." Cf. also Exodus xxxii, 32, 33, and Psalm 69, 28. There are many mentions of the Book of Life, in the singular, but not in the plural. The plural here has been thought to be due to an error of the person who wrote down from Milton's dictation.

366. *Through God's high sufferance . . . man.* An idea like that expressed in 211–213, but there God's purpose in leaving Satan at liberty was that he should further incriminate

himself, whereas here it is to test man ("for the trial of man").

368. *corrupted* is completed by three clauses—(1) "to for-sake" (368); (2) "to transform" (370); (3) "to adore" (373), each marking a result of the corruption—'so that they forsook' ... 'transformed' ... 'adored.'

This passage resembles St Paul's Epistle to the Romans (i, 23), "[Men] changed the glory of the uncor-rupted God into an image like to corruptible man, and to birds, and four-footed beasts, and creeping things." But St Paul blames man himself, and does not mention the part played by Satan and his angels.

372. *religions*, 'religious rites.' That anything connected with religion should be "gay" would have seemed out-rageous to a Puritan.

372. *full of pomp and gold*. Milton came to dislike all pomp and splendour in ritual; for instance he speaks with scorn of the "gaudy copes and painted windows" in the royal chapel (*Eikonoklastes* xxv) though in *Il Penseroso* he took a different view. (*Il Penseroso*, 155–166.)

376–521. In making this long list of pagan gods Milton doubtless had in mind the Catalogue of Ships with their captains in Homer (*Iliad* II, 484 *ff.*) and Virgil's list of the chieftains who fought against Aeneas (*Aeneid* VII, 641 *ff.*), and like Homer and Virgil he begins with an invocation of the Muses. See also Introduction, p. 12.

The fallen angels, now under the names of pagan gods, are divided into classes, according to the districts in which they were worshipped. These are (1) the Holy Land itself (381–418); (2) Syria and Phoenicia (419–476); (3) Egypt (476–489); (4) Belial, with no special sanc-tuary (490–505); (5) Greece and Rome (557–521).

In the *Nativity Ode* (173–228) there is a list of divini-ties rather like this, but shorter; they are the various pagan gods and spirits which perished at the birth of

Christ. Many of them are the same as those mentioned here, *e.g.*, Moloch, Peor, Ashtaroth, Thammuz, etc. It is interesting to compare the two passages, which have much in common but are very different in tone.

378. *next in worth* after Satan himself and Beelzebub, or perhaps 'in order of dignity.'

380. *promiscuous*, 'mixed,' 'confused.'

381 *ff*. First came the angels who were the bolde stand dared to settle in the Holy Land itself.

382. *Roaming to seek their prey, cf*. I Peter v, 8: "The devil, as a roaring lion, walketh about, seeking whom he may devour."

382. *durst fix . . . by his altar*. The impious kings Manasseh and Ahaz were guilty of this sacrilege (II Kings xxi, 4, 5, and xvi, 10 *ff*.).

385. *abide*, 'endure,' 'face.'

386. *thundering*. Thunder is often regarded as the voice of God in scripture, *e.g.*, Psalm 77, 18 and Psalm 81, 7.

387. *Between the Cherubim*. There were two golden figures of cherubim one on each side of the 'Mercy Seat' above the Ark of the Covenant.

389. *Abominations*. The tremendous emphasis agrees with the frequent and emphatic use of the word in the scriptures, when the sins of the Israelites, especially the worship of idols, are denounced. *E.g.*, Jeremiah vii, 30, Ezekiel vii, 20, viii, 6, 9, and elsewhere.

391. *affront* is very likely another instance of a double meaning: (1) 'Insult,' as now generally used, (2) 'confront,' 'face,' the older meaning as in Shakespeare, *Hamlet* III, i, 29–31:

> For we have closely sent for Hamlet hither,
> That he, as 'twere by accident, may here
> Affront Ophelia.

—when certainly no 'insult' was planned.

392. *Moloch* means 'king,' and Milton often gives him that title—*e.g.*, II, 43, "sceptred king," *Nativity Ode* 209, "the grisly king."

He is often mentioned in the Old Testament, and was a god of the Ammonites, who cruelly sacrificed children to him by means of his brass statue, which contained a furnace. Their cries were drowned by the "drums and timbrels." The worship of Moloch is described in Sandys' *Travels*, a book well known in Milton's day. Milton also speaks of Moloch in the *Nativity Ode*, 205–210:

> And sullen Moloch, fled,
> Hath left in shadows dread
>   His burning idol all of blackest hue;
> In vain with cymbals' ring
> They call the grisly King,
>   In dismal dance about the furnace blue.

397. *Rabba* (Rabbah), the capital of the Ammonites, called in II Samuel xii, 27 "the city of waters"; hence "her watery plain." Rabbah was captured by David.

398. *Argob* and *Basan* (Bashan) were in the kingdom of Og, whose defeat by the Israelites is narrated in Deuteronomy iii, 1–13. They were on the east bank of the Jordan and the Sea of Galilee. Milton places them further south, and regards them as being in the territory of the Ammonites, probably by an inference from the passage of Deuteronomy.

Milton regularly uses forms in *s* rather than in *sh*, as "Basan" here, "Chemos" (406), "Hesebon" (408), "Sittim" (413), instead of "Bashan," "Chemosh," "Heshbon," "Shittim," as in the Authorized Version of the Bible. The forms in *s* are used in the Septuagint and the Vulgate, and no doubt Milton preferred the less harsh sound.

400. *Audacious* because so near to the Holy Land.

400. *the wisest heart/Of Solomon.* The wisdom of Solomon is proverbial. For the original account, see I Kings iv, 29–34.

Solomon was won over by his idolatrous wives in his old age, and built "an high place" for Chemosh and Moloch (I Kings xi, 4–8) on the peaks of the Mount of Olives, which was therefore called "the Mount of Corruption" (II Kings xxiii, 13) or "the Mount of Offence" (hence "that opprobrious hill"). The groves of Moloch and other heathen gods are mentioned by Jeremiah.

The valley of Hinnom was a pleasant place, once a royal garden, and watered by the brook which flowed from the pool of Siloam. After the sacrifices to Moloch had taken place here, the valley was regarded with horror, and the Greek form of its name, 'Gehenna,' came to mean Hell. "Tophet" is another name for the same place, and is said to be derived from a Hebrew word meaning 'cymbal' or 'drum,' in allusion to the "drums and timbrels" used in the rites of Moloch. All these sacrifices and rituals were ended by Josiah, who destroyed the 'high places,' cut down the 'groves,' and put a curse upon the place, ordering it to be used for the disposal of every sort of rubbish and garbage. (II Kings xxiii, 10–14.)

403. *that,* 'the well-known.'

406. *Chemos,* (= Chemosh) was the Moabite equivalent of Moloch. Another name for the same god was Peor (412) or Baal-Peor.

407–414. The places here mentioned are on the east side of the river Jordan and of the Dead Sea; the country had at various times belonged to the Moabites, the Ammonites, the Amorites, and the tribe of Reuben. The exact situation of the various places as understood in Milton's time is often doubtful, as the maps of that time differ greatly from ours and even from one another—

e.g., the Abarim mountains are sometimes placed north
of the river Arnon, sometimes south of it, while Nebo
is sometimes a town and sometimes a mountain; the
river Arnon is placed sometimes near the north end of
the Dead Sea, sometimes about half-way down it, sometimes even far away, to the north-west of Rabba, not
reaching the Dead Sea at all. However, Milton was not
a geographer but a poet, and probably he took little
interest in details of situation (if indeed any one claimed
to know them exactly) but thought first of all of the
scriptural association of the places, and of the sound of
their names in verse.

All the cities were captured by the Israelites, their
gods being therefore defeated by Jehovah.

Most of the places named occur in the lament for
Moab in Isaiah xv and xvi.

407. *Aroer* is near the northern bank of the Arnon.

407. *Nebo* is usually said to be a headland of the high
plateau of the Abarim range, but it is also shown as a
town on some old maps.

408. *southmost Abarim*. On some old maps the Abarim
mountains are represented as lying south of the river
Arnon, stretching to the southern border of Moab.
Milton may have had this in mind.

408. *Hesebon*, (Heshbon) north-east of Mount Nebo and
not far from it. It is often mentioned as the city of Sihon
(Seon), King of the Amorites (Numbers xxi, 26) a
notable enemy defeated by the Israelites.

409. *Horonaim* was in the territory of Moab, but its exact
site is not known.

409. *Seon* = Sihon, King of the Amorites.

410. *Sibma*. Its vines are mentioned in Isaiah xiv, 8–10, and
Jeremiah xlviii, 32.

411. *Eleale*, a town near Heshbon.

411. *the Asphaltic Pool*: the Dead Sea, in ancient times called

Lake Asphaltites because of the lumps of asphalt (bitumen) which float upon its surface.

412. *Peor:* Baal-Peor. The Israelites were induced by the Moabite women to take part in the worship of Baal-Peor in Shittim (Numbers xxv, 1–3). In the *Nativity Ode* (197–198) Milton says, "Peor and Baalim/Forsake their temples dim" (at the birth of Christ). Baal (plural 'Baalim') was the chief god of the Canaanites, worshipped under several local names, Baal-Peor being the Baal worshipped at Peor.

413. *Sittim* = Shittim, east of the Jordan, on the other bank of which is Jericho.

413. *Nile, i.e.,* Egypt.

414. *which cost them woe.* Numbers xxv, 9, "Those that died in the plague [sent by God in punishment for the worship of Baal-Peor] were twenty and four thousand."

415. *orgies:* enthusiastic rites usually secret, in honour of a god. By their nature they were liable to become immoral 'orgies' in the modern sense.

415. *enlarged,* 'spread further' that is, to Jerusalem itself.

416. *hill of scandal,* the "opprobrious hill" of 403, where Solomon built a 'high place' for Chemosh as well as for Moloch.

416. *the grove/Of Moloch. Cf.* 403.

418. *good Josiah.* The destruction of the heathen altars, 'high places,' etc. and their priests by Josiah is described in II Kings xxiii, 1–20, and II Chronicles xxxiv, 1–7.

419. *the bordering flood,* because the Euphrates marked the extreme eastern limit of Palestine as promised by God (Genesis xv, 18).

420. *Euphrates.* It was one of the four rivers which flowed from the Garden of Eden (Genesis ii, 14).

420. *the brook:* "the river of Egypt" (Genesis xv, 18), called in I Samuel xxx, 10, "the brook Besor." It is in fact a small stream which dries up in summer.

422. *Baalim*. See note on 412.

422. *Ashtaroth* is plural, the singular being "Ashtoreth." ("Astoreth" in 438) but the distinction is not always made. She was the female counterpart of Baal; they are often mentioned together.

423–431. This description of the powers of spirits would not have seemed at all surprising to Milton's readers in his own day, for such topics were often discussed with much interest. Though it seems to us at first sight a digression, much of it proves to be of importance to the story of *Paradise Lost*. Milton repeats some of the details in Book VI (352 *ff.*):

> . . . and as they please,
> They limb themselves, and colour, shape, or size
> Assume, as likes them best, condense or rare.

425. *essence pure:* the "empyreal substance" *cf.* line 17 (where see note).

426. *manacled*, 'fettered.'

427. *brittle strength*. A contradiction in terms, yet both are true.

428. *in what shape they choose*. Later (777–795) we shall see that the fallen angels shrank from gigantic into minute shapes in order to fit into Satan's hall. Satan himself takes a variety of shapes in *Paradise Lost*; for example when spying on Adam and Eve he becomes first a lion, then a tiger. (IV, 401–403.) And, most notable of all, he becomes the serpent which caused their downfall.

429. *Dilated*, 'expanded,' 'rarefied.' *Cf.* quotation in note on 423–431.

429. *obscure*, 'dark.'

432–437. See for example Judges ii, 11–15.

433. *their living Strength:* God. *Cf.* I Samuel xv, 29, "the Strength of Israel will not lie." And "the living God" frequently in the Bible.

435. *bestial gods*, such as the golden calf (Exodus xxxii, 1–8) and the Egyptian gods in the form of beasts.

436. *Bowed down* ironically repeats "bowing lowly down" of 434.

438. *Astoreth:* the most important of the Ashtaroth. She was a moon-goddess worshipped in Phoenicia. In the *Nativity Ode* (200–204) she is called "mooned Ashtaroth," and "Heaven's Queen" since among her titles was 'Queen of Heaven.'

439. *with crescent horns* because in her statues she was represented with the crescent moon, which looks like horns, upon her head.

441. *Sidonian*, 'Phoenician,' Sidon being the chief city of Phoenicia.

442–446. Solomon was persuaded by his foreign wives to worship strange gods, among them Ashtoreth (I Kings xi, 5). For this passage see note on 400.

443. *the offensive mountain*, called "that opprobrious hill" in 403.

444. *though large.* Solomon's "largeness of heart" is mentioned along with his wisdom in I Kings iv, 29.

446. *Thammuz*, the son of a Syrian king, was beloved by Ashtoreth. He was killed by a boar which he was hunting, but Ashtoreth persuaded the gods of the lower world to allow him to spend half the year on earth with her, the other half being spent in the world below. The Phoenician women held a ceremony of mourning for him every year, a custom which spread to other countries; Ezekiel (viii, 14) saw the women of Israel "weeping for Tammuz" at the very door of the Temple, and the Greeks adopted the story, transferring it to Adonis and Aphrodite, the Greek counterparts of Thammuz and Ashtoreth. The custom was probably in reality a lament for the death of the year, or what is called a 'vegetation myth.' Milton refers to the custom also in

the *Nativity Ode*, 204, "In vain the Tyrian maids their wounded Thammuz mourn."

450. *smooth*, 'flowing smoothly.'

450. *native* because the river had its source in Lebanon.

451. *Ran purple to the sea.* The river Adonis is said to become red at certain seasons because of the red deposit washed down from the mountains of Lebanon.

453. *heat*, 'passion.'

455. *by the vision led.* Although far away in captivity, Ezekiel saw in a vision the evil deeds of the Israelites.

456. *dark idolatries*—Ezekiel viii, 12. "Hast thou seen what the ancients of the house of Israel do in the dark, every man in the chambers of his imagery?"

458. *Who mourned in earnest*, in contrast to the theatrical mourning for Thammuz. The story is told in I Samuel v, 1–4. The Philistines captured the Ark, and put it in the temple of Dagon at Ashdod. In the morning the idol of Dagon was found fallen on the ground before the Ark, the head and hands lying on the threshold of the temple.

460. *grunsel* = ground-sill ('threshold'). *Cf.* 'window-sill.'

462. *Dagon:* the chief god of the Philistines. He has been regarded as a fish-god, the lower part of his body being that of a fish. In the margin of I Samuel i, 4 in the Authorized Version the words "the stump of Dagon" are alternatively translated "the fishy part." In *Samson Agonistes*, 13, Milton speaks of "Dagon, their sea-idol."

464. *Azotus*, the Greek form of 'Ashdod.'

464–466. Azotus, Gath, Ascalon, Accaron (Ekron), and Gaza were the chief cities of the Philistines.

466. *frontier bounds, i.e.,* the southern boundary of the land of Canaan. (Genesis x, 19.)

467. *Rimmon:* a Syrian god.

468. *Damascus* was famous for the beauty of its situation and its fertile soil; it is still an important city.

469. *Abbana* (Abana) and *Pharphar* (Pharpar) are often mentioned both in the Bible and by later travellers as being the feature of the city.

469. *lucid*, 'shining' or 'clear.'

471. *A leper:* Naaman, captain of the Syrian army, who went to Elisha to be cured of leprosy. Elisha commanded him to bathe in the river Jordan, which he at first refused to do, saying that the rivers Abana and Pharpar were better than the Jordan. But having been persuaded to obey, he was cured, and forthwith embraced the Hebrew religion. (II Kings v, 1–19.)

472. Ahaz persuaded the King of Assyria to capture Damascus, and later went there to meet him. At Damascus he saw an altar, of which he had a copy made and set up in front of the Temple at Jerusalem; on his return he removed the 'brazen altar' and substituted the other, on which he sacrificed. (II Kings xvi, 10–15.) He also worshipped the gods of Damascus (II Chronicles xxviii, 23).

472. *sottish*, 'foolish.'

473. *disparage*, 'insult.'

477. *crew*, 'a crowd'—usually contemptuous in Milton.

477. *of old renown, i.e.*, from the point of view of Milton's own (and our own) day, not of course from that of the fallen angels.

478. *Osiris:* the chief god of the Egyptians. He was a king of Egypt, who, having civilized his own country, travelled to others to spread civilization. Having returned, he was murdered by his brother Set, or Typhon, who cut up his body and scattered the pieces. Isis found them and embalmed them, after which Osiris came to life again, and reigned as king over the living and judge of the dead.

478. *Isis:* sister and wife of Osiris.

478. *Orus* (Horus): son of Isis and Osiris.

479. *With monstrous shapes.* The Egyptian gods were represented as partly animals in form, Isis for instance had the horns of a cow, Horus the head of a hawk, while Osiris was regarded as actually incarnate in the form of the bull Apis, which was kept in the temple of Osiris at Memphis. Many animals were regarded as sacred, *e.g.*, cats, crocodiles, etc., while others were supposed to be protected or even inhabited by gods.

Milton enumerates the Egyptian gods in the *Nativity Ode*, 211–215:

> The brutish gods of Nile as fast,
> Isis and Orus and the dog Anubis, haste.

> Nor is Osiris seen
> In Memphian grove or green,
> Trampling the unshowered grass with lowings loud.

479. *abused*, 'deceived.' Its opposite, 'disabuse,' still means undeceive.'

481. *wandering gods.* The Roman poets Ovid and Juvenal relate a story that when the giants made war on the gods (see note on 198) some of the gods fled to Egypt and disguised themselves as animals. Milton would have known this story, and probably has it in mind here.

483. *borrowed gold.* Milton suggests that the golden calf (Exodus xxxii, 1–8) was made out of the jewellery which the Israelites borrowed from the Egyptians before they left Egypt (Exodus xii, 35); also that the golden calf was a direct imitation of the Egyptian animal gods. It is not improbable that the Israelites were familiar with the idea from their long stay in Egypt, and inclined to adopt it themselves.

484. *the rebel king:* Jeroboam, who rebelled against Solomon's successor Rehoboam, and set up a kingdom for himself in the north of Palestine. At Bethel and Dan, cities near the frontier, he set up golden calves, so "doubling" the sin. (I Kings xii, 28 *ff.*)

486. *Cf.* Psalm 106, 20 (of the golden calf), "They changed their glory into the similitude of an ox that eateth grass."

487. *he:* Jehovah, in the form of his chosen people.

488. *marching, cf.* Exodus vi, 26, "the Lord said, 'Bring out the children of Israel from the land of Egypt according to their armies'." So also Exodus vii, 4 and xii, 51.

488. *equalled,* Gods, men and animals are all made equal by death. This was the tenth plague sent upon Egypt, by which all the first-born, whether men or animals, were killed. See Exodus xii, 12 and 29.

489. *her bleating gods:* the Egyptian gods, with their animal forms and attributes, or the sacred animals themselves. God "executed judgement" on the gods of Egypt as well as on man and beast. (Exodus xii, 12, Numbers xxxiii, 4.) "Bleating" covers any animal noise, but the word is used with great contempt as applied to "gods" —bleating being perhaps the most ridiculous of animal sounds.

490. *Belial,* in the Old Testament, is not the name of any actual god, but is an abstract term meaning 'worthlessness,' or 'wickedness' in general; the phrase "sons" or "children" of Belial is often applied to those who are called in a marginal note "naughty men" (Deuteronomy xiii, 13). In the New Testament however, "Belial" is a proper name, though still not that of any local god, but of the spirit of evil in general (II Corinthians vi, 15, "What concord hath Christ with Belial?").

490. *last,* but certainly not least. The end of a procession is as important as the beginning, and Belial corresponds to Moloch in importance, while his opposite in character. Read the description of them in Book II, 43–50 (Moloch) and 109–118 (Belial).

492. *no temple,* because he was not a local god.

493–494. Milton's religious and political opinions naturally incline him to find Belial in the Church as then constituted and in the court of Charles II, to which line 497 would readily be understood to apply.

495. *Eli's sons*, priests of God at Shiloh, whose misdeeds are recounted in I Samuel ii, 12–17.

497. *Cf. Paradise Regained* II, 182–183:

> Have we not seen, or by relation heard,
> In courts and regal chambers how thou lurkst?

(Satan, speaking of Belial)

500. *injury*, 'injustice.'

500–505. This may well be aimed at the dissolute courtiers of Charles II, to whom the Puritans often referred as "Sons of Belial."

502. *flown*, a variant of 'flowed,' *i.e.*, 'flooded'; 'overflown' in this sense occurs several times in Spenser and elsewhere.

503–505. Refers to Genesis xix and Judges xix.

506. *prime*, 'chief.' *Cf.* II, 423.

507. *The rest . . . tell.* 'It would take a long time to mention all the others'—a sentence adopted by many later writers from classical authors. Milton says he will not stop to mention all the other fallen angels who became gods of the heathen, but he briefly enumerates some of the Greek gods, because of their importance in the history of culture and of his own special interest in Greek mythology.

508. *Ionian*: Greek. The Ionians, one of the chief divisions of the Greek people, were supposed to be descended from Javan ("Javan's issue"), son of Japheth son of Noah; the "isles of the Gentiles" (*i.e.*, the Greek islands) were divided among his sons. (Genesis x, 2–5.)

508. *of*, 'by.'

508. *held*, 'considered.'

509. *confessed*, 'admitted to be.'

510. *Titan*, see note on 198. Here, however, Milton gives a rather different version of the myth, speaking of a

single god called Titan instead of the twelve Titans, and making Saturn rebel against him (presumably an elder brother) instead of against his father Uranus.

The eldest of the Titans is usually said to be Oceanus, whose children included 3000 rivers and 3000 ocean nymphs—an "enormous brood" indeed, in the present-day sense of the word 'enormous,' though Milton probably meant 'monstrous.'

513. *Rhea:* sister and wife of Saturn, mother of Zeus (Jove).

513. *like measure,* 'the same treatment.'

514–521. Strictly speaking, the construction of this paragraph is irregular: "These first . . . ruled the middle air, their highest Heaven" is followed by the mention of various places, with no verb, but presumably one should be understood from "ruled"; the last clause, introduced by "or who," has no clear grammatical connexion with what goes before. But in spite of these irregularities the reader is led on from one clause to the next without difficulty.

514. *Crete* was the birthplace of Zeus (Jove).

515. *Ida:* a mountain in Crete.

515. *snowy top.* Homer calls Mount Olympus "snowy."

516. *Olympus,* regarded by the Greeks as the home of the gods, is a mountain in northern Greece. It is very high and its peak is often snow-covered even in summer.

516. *middle air.* This probably refers to a medieval theory that the air was divided into three regions, of which the lowest was warm and damp, the uppermost hot, and the middle one cold; this last extended as far as the tops of the highest mountains (such as Olympus), and in it clouds and rain were formed.

517. *Delphian cliff.* The famous oracle of Apollo was at Delphi, on the edge of a deep and precipitous ravine high on Mount Parnassus.

518. *Dodona,* in Epirus, was the seat of an oracle of Zeus.

519. *Doric land:* Greece. The Dorians, one of the races composing the Greek people, lived in the country called Doris.

519. *Saturn,* when defeated by Zeus, fled to Italy. The 'Golden Age' was believed to correspond to his reign.

520. *Adria:* the Adriatic sea.

520. *Hesperian fields:* Italy ("Hesperian" = 'Western,' Italy being the western land to the Greeks).

521. *Celtic (sc.* 'fields'): France. For "fields" = 'land' *cf. Comus,* 60, "Roving the Celtic and Iberian fields."

521. *the utmost isles:* Britain. "Utmost" = 'furthest.' The British Islands were thought of by the ancients as being on the very edge of the earth.

523. *damp,* 'depressed.' We still speak of a thing being 'damping' or 'damping to one's spirit.'

523. *such, sc.* 'looks.'

525–526. *not lost/In loss itself,* 'not utterly lost.'

526. *which,* i.e., the 'looks' of his followers, downcast but yet with signs of joy. "His" is emphatic—Satan's.

528. *recollecting,* ('re-collecting') summoning up again.

528–529. *that bore/Semblance of worth, not substance.* Milton here warns the reader that Satan's courage, the way he heartens his subordinates and the wonderful military show they are about to put up, however magnificent outwardly, are yet rotten within.

534. *Azazel* is here probably a demon mentioned by some medieval writers, one of whom says he is one of four standard-bearers. The name occurs first in Leviticus xvi, 8, where it is translated as "scapegoat" in the Authorized Version.

536. *advanced,* 'raised,' as in V, 588.

538. *emblazed* ('emblazoned'). A term in heraldry, meaning 'adorned with heraldic devices.'

539. *Seraphic,* 'belonging to the angels'—their various coats of arms, etc.

540. Notice the deep vowel sounds, suggesting the notes of the trumpets. (This phrase is an 'absolute' construction with no verb.)

542. *Hell's concave:* the vaulted roof of Hell, *cf.* "vaulted with fire" (298) and "the cope of Hell" (345).

543. *reign,* 'kingdom,' the Latin *regnum.*

Chaos was king of the realm of Chaos, and Night was his queen, *cf.* II, 959-963, where Night is also called "eldest of things."

546. *orient,* 'bright.' It first means 'eastern' (from the rising sun), then 'bright' (like the colours of sunrise).

548. *serried,* 'locked together' (from the French word *serrer*).

550. *phalanx:* a peculiarly strong, compact military formation used in the Macedonian army of Alexander the Great and others.

550. *Dorian mood.* "Mood" = 'mode.' Greek music was composed in one of three 'modes'—the Dorian, the Phrygian, or the Lydian. The difference between them can best be described as resembling the difference between major and minor in our music. The Dorian mode was simple and solemn, according to Plato (*Rep.* III, 273-274) "the only one suitable for warlike and temperate men," the Phrygian was exciting and martial, the Lydian soft and sweet.

551-555. It is usually said that Milton is thinking of Thucydides' description (II, 157) of the Spartan advance at the battle of Mantinea; the Argives moved swiftly, inspired by rage, but the Spartans marched slowly, to the music of flutes, in order to keep their ranks steady and unbroken.

553. *instead of rage.* When Satan needed to rouse the spirits of his followers to action, he made us of "trumpets loud and clarions" (532); but now steadiness and determination is wanted, for which "flutes and soft recorders" are more appropriate.

554. *breathed*, 'inspired.'

555. *With*, 'by.'

556. *swage*, 'assuage,' 'soothe.'

561. *to*, 'to the sound of.'

561. *charmed, i.e.*, made their steps less painful. *Cf.* II, 566:

> . . . could charm
> Pain for a while.

562. *the burnt soil*, cf. 228–229, 296.

563. *horrid* probably in its original Latin sense of "bristling" (with spears, etc.).

565. *ordered* is a military term. Arms are 'ordered' when soldiers halt, and rest their weapons upright on the ground at their sides.

567–569. *files* are rows of soldiers one behind the other (while in 'ranks' they are side by side). At the present time soldiers are drawn up on parade in ranks, with files of only two deep, each file separated by a space from the one behind it. But formerly files might be of any depth. We may picture Satan's forces as being drawn up in open order, so that as he walked along the front of his troops ("traverse") he could look between the angels all the way down their files.

Milton, having lived through the civil wars, knew the details of military drill.

572. *his* probably = 'its' here, *i.e.*, his heart's. See note on 254.

573–587. Milton here enumerates all the greatest and most famous armies which might be compared with Satan's host (to their disadvantage)—the giants of Greek mythology, the heroes of the Theban and Trojan legends, the Knights of the Round Table, and the Paladins of the medieval romances. He uses all these names of places to produce an atmosphere of high romance, and chooses those which do so by their mere sound, even if you do not happen to know where they were—though it adds to the interest if you do. Milton himself was deeply interested in, and familiar with, both the classical legends and the medieval romances; as he says in the *Apology for Smectymnuus*, "That I may tell you whither my younger feet wandered; I betook me among those lofty fables and romances, which recount in solemn cantos the deeds of knighthood founded by our victorious kings; and from hence had in renown over all Christendom."

573. *since created man.* A Latin form of speech, where we should now say 'since the creation of man.' *Cf. Comus,* 48, "after the Tuscan mariners transformed"—'after the transformation of the Tuscan mariners.' Latin preferred concrete to abstract expressions.

574. *embodied,* 'assembled.'

574. *named,* 'compared.'

575. *Could merit more* probably means that compared with Satan's host no army that could be gathered together would be of more importance than if they were a race of pygmies. But it may mean that no such army would deserve a better fate than that of the Pygmies, namely to be constantly defeated, as the Pygmies were by the cranes.

575. *that small infantry:* the Pygmies, a race of dwarfs who according to Homer (*Iliad* III, 5-6), were constantly attacked by flocks of migrating cranes. The medieval geographers still believed in their existence, and mark their home on maps as being in central Asia. Milton refers to this in 780:

> . . . that pygmaean race
> Beyond the Indian mount

577. *Phlegra,* later called Pallene, is the westernmost of the three peninsulas of the Chalcidice, in northern Greece. The battle between the gods and the giants was said to have taken place there.

578. *Thebes:* the centre of the stories of the Oedipus cycle, made famous by plays of Aeschylus, Sophocles, and Euripides. Milton speaks of these legends in *Il Penseroso*, 97–100:

> Sometime let gorgeous Tragedy
> In sceptred pall come sweeping by,
> Presenting Thebes, or Pelops' line,
> Or the tale of Troy divine.

578. *Ilium*, another name for Troy, celebrated in Homer's *Iliad* and Virgil's *Aeneid*, and by many other ancient writers.

579. *auxiliar gods.* Gods and goddesses took part in all these battles, either in their own proper persons or in disguise.

580. *fable:* chronicles such as those of Geoffrey of Monmouth.

580. *romance*, such as Malory's *Morte d'Arthur.*

580. *Uther's son:* King Arthur, son of Uther Pendragon. Milton had originally intended his great work to be an epic on the subject of King Arthur.

581. *Begirt with*, 'surrounded by.'

581. *Armoric.* Armorica was another name for what we now call Brittany. Brittany was closely connected with Britain in the Arthurian legends.

582. *baptized or infidel*, 'Christian or Saracen.' We now come to the romances concerning Charlemagne and his Paladins.

583. *Jousted*, 'fought in tournaments.'
    The names of places which follow here were all famous from their mention in the numerous romances, mostly Italian, about Charlemagne.

583. *Aspramont.* There are several places of this or similar names—one in the Netherlands, one near Nice in Southern France, and one a range of mountains in Calabria in southern Italy. The last is probably the one referred to here. Charlemagne encountered the Saracens

near Reggio, their base, and was nearly slain by a Saracen prince, being rescued by Roland. Mercator's map, of Milton's time, shows a town called Aspramont in the Calabrian mountains and one called Aspremont near Nice.

583. *Montalban*, in Languedoc (southern France), is mentioned in several of the romances. It belonged to Renaud (Rinaldo) who was besieged there by Charlemagne.

584. *Damasco*, the medieval form of 'Damascus,' used here by Milton because he is thinking of it in connexion with the romances; when thinking of it in connexion with scripture he uses its older and scriptural form 'Damascus' (468).

584. *Marocco*. We now call it 'Morocco.' The name recalls wars between Moors and Spaniards.

584. *Trebisond* (Trebizond, or Trapezus) in Asia Minor was the seat of an empire in the thirteenth to fifteenth centuries. It was celebrated for its magnificence and for the tournaments held there. Scott refers to it in *Ivanhoe*.

585. *Biserta:* Bizerta, on the Tunisian coast, from which the King of Africa set out to attack Charlemagne's troops in France.

586. Milton's version of this legend is rather different from that generally current. There were however many romances and chronicles which he may be following; the *Song of Roland*, which is now far the most famous of these, was not known in Milton's day. According to this, the Saracens, by the help of a traitor, fell upon the rearguard of Charlemagne's army in the pass of Roncesvalles. Roland carried a horn which he was to blow if he should need help, but he refused to do so until it was too late, with the result that he himself and almost all his men perished. Charlemagne, on hearing the horn, returned and put the Saracens to flight. Neither he nor

the rest of the Paladins was killed in the battle; in fact he himself lived for many years after it. Scott refers to the story in *Marmion* (VI, 30):

> O for a blast of that dread horn
> On Fontarabian echoes borne,
> That to King Charles did come,
> When Rowland brave, and Olivier,
> And every paladin and peer,
> On Ronces valley died.

586. *peerage*, 'peers,' the twelve 'pairs' or 'paladins,' of whom Roland and Oliver were the chief.

587. *Fontarabbia*. It is not known why Milton introduces the name of this place, as it is many miles from Ronces-valles, the actual place of battle. He may have got the information from some Spanish historian.

Fontarabbia (now Fuenterrabia) was a fortress on the frontier between Spain and France.

588. *observed*, 'obeyed.' The fallen angels, though far above all the great warriors just mentioned, yet acknowledged the superior authority of Satan himself.

591–592. *his form . . . brightness*. Before his fall, Satan was radiant with light ("glory"), and still kept some of this brightness. As he goes on from evil to evil, his brightness decreases. Some has already been lost, as this passage shows (and *cf.* 97, "though changed in outward lustre"); later (IV, 835), the cherub Zephon says to him:

> Think not, revolted spirit, thy shape the same,
> Or undiminished brightness, to be known,
> As when thou stood'st in heaven upright and pure;
> That glory then, when thou no more wast good,
> Departed from thee.

And Gabriel speaks of his "faded splendour wan" (IV, 870). As yet he has not sunk so low, but still retains some of his brightness.

597. *disastrous*, foreboding disaster. Notice who the word stands out, suggesting the terror caused by the darkness. The word 'disaster' originally had an astrological meaning, that of a dangerous position of the stars (*aster* is Greek for 'star'); some trace of this meaning may still be felt here. We still sometimes use the word 'ill-starred,' generally without thinking of its original meaning.

Before the days of scientific astronomy eclipses were very naturally believed to be portents of evil to come.

598–599. *with fear of change|Perplexes monarchs*. This sentence is said to have been regarded as a threat to Charles II, and nearly to have prevented the publication of *Paradise Lost*.

601. *thunder:* the weapon of God. *Cf.* 93.

601. *intrenched*, 'cut into.'

603. *considerate*, 'thoughtful,' 'deliberate.'

604. *Waiting revenge*, as Satan had said in his speech to Beelzebub,

> All is not lost: the unconquerable will,
> And study of revenge, immortal hate,
> And courage never to submit or yield.

604. *Waiting*, 'waiting for.'

605. *remorse* here perhaps in the sense of 'pity,' though the repetition of "his" in lines 608 and 611 suggests a troubled conscience.

605. *passion*, deep feeling, not anger as usually now.

606. *fellows*, 'companions' or 'partners' in his crime.

609. *amerced*. A legal word, meaning 'to punish,' or more particularly 'to fine.' Here 'punished by the loss of Heaven.'

611. *yet faithful how they stood* depends on "O behold" (605).

612–615. One of the older critics, Newton, points out how strikingly appropriate this simile is:

It represents the majestic stature and withered glory of the Angels: and the last with great propriety, since their lustre was impaired by thunder, as well as that of the trees in the simile: and besides, the blasted heath gives us some idea of that singed burning soil, on which the Angels were standing.

613. *scathed*, 'injured.'

615. *the blasted heath* reminds us of that on which Macbeth encountered the witches (Shakespeare, *Macbeth* I, iii, 77).

616. *doubled . . . bend, i.e.*, they bend their ranks so as to make them double ('proleptic' use).

616-618. *their doubled ranks . . . peers*. The army of angels now forms a semi-circle round Satan and his immediate followers, in order to hear him better.

619. *assayed*, 'essayed,' 'tried.'

619. *thrice*, very much more effective than merely 'often' would have been. *Cf.* "nine times" (50).

622. As in his first speech (84-124), Satan is somewhat incoherent, there from anger, here from pity and remorse. In particular, lines 622-626 cannot be logically explained, though their general drift is clear enough.

623. *Matchless but with the Almighty*, 'not to be compared to any but the Almighty.'

623. *that strife*. "That" is emphatic—the strife implied by "matchless."

624. *event*, 'result,' 'outcome.'

629-630. *How . . . could.* We should say 'that . . . would.'

631. *loss, sc.* 'of the battle'; 'defeat.'

632. *exile*, with the second syllable accented, as always in Milton.

633. *Hath emptied Heaven*. An exaggeration, since according to Satan himself only a third of the angels followed him (V, 710). This was the accepted tradition suggested by Revelation xii, 4.

634. *Self-raised*. So Moloch in II, 75-81 points out that upward movement is the natural one for angels, and great

force was needed to drive them down, so that "the ascent is easy."

635–637. Satan is trying to shift the blame by implying that the plan was not his but theirs.

635. *all the host of Heaven*, meaning the fallen angels only, a flattering way of addressing them.

636. *counsels different or dangers shunned.* Again a Latin use of the concrete where we should use the abstract—'my holding different opinions from the rest, and avoiding dangers.'

641. *still*, 'always.' *Cf.* 68, *note.*

642. *tempted our attempt.* Puns and jingles of this sort occur frequently in literature of this period, and also in classical literature and even in the Bible. We now regard a pun as a rather poor kind of joke, but this was not at all the intention in these instances; nothing funny was intended, but rather a special emphasis or rhetorical ornament. Another instance occurs in II, 39–40, "Surer to prosper than prosperity/Could have assured us."

645. *provoked*, 'when it has been provoked.'

646. *work*, 'effect,' 'achieve.'

646. *close*, 'secret.'

647. *no less* can bear two possible meanings—(1) God shall learn from us, just as we learnt from him by experience; (2) no less than if we used force.

650 *ff.* Satan himself here gives a rough outline of the plan which he ultimately carried out. Beelzebub goes into greater detail about it in his speech in II, 345 *ff.* and Satan again in II, 830–835.

650. *rife*, 'prevalent.'

651. *fame*, 'rumour,' the Latin meaning. *Cf.* II, 346, "If ancient and prophetic fame in heaven/Err not."

655. *if but to pry.* This is just what he did when he reached the earth—"and pry/In every bush and brake." (IX, 159.)

656. *eruption*, 'sortie'—their first expedition outside Hell.

658. *the Abyss:* Chaos, as in 21.

659. *cover*, *sc.* celestial spirits.

660. *peace is despaired*, 'despaired of.' Another Latin form of speech. *Cf.* VI, 495, "Think nothing hard, much less to be despaired."

661. *think submission*, 'think of.'

662. *understood*, *sc.* 'between ourselves,' that is to say 'secret.' For the sense *cf.* II, 187, "War . . . open or concealed."

667–668. The Roman soldiers applauded the speeches of their generals in this way.

671. *the rest entire*, 'all the rest' (of the hill).

672. *scurf*, 'incrustation.'

673. *his*, 'its' (the hill's).

674. *The work of sulphur.* Bacon, the great scientific authority at this time, says "Mercury and sulphur are the principal materials of metals." (*Nat. Hist.* IV, 354.) This was the accepted theory. The heat of sulphur was supposed to turn earth into metals.

675. *brigad*, so spelled by Milton, and pronounced with the accent on the first syllable.

676. *pioners* strictly means 'foot-soldiers' but is used particularly of sappers and miners, who clear the way for the main army, dig trenches, etc. The forms *pioner* and *enginer* etc. for *pioneer* and *engineer* were common in seventeenth-century English. See *Hamlet* III, iv, 206–207, "For 'tis the sport to have the enginer/Hoist with his own petar."

677. *camp* here means 'army.'

678. *Mammon* really means 'riches,' and occurs in this sense in the Bible, but the word was later taken to mean the god of riches. *Cf.* the use of 'Belial' (490 *note*). Spenser made this personification in his description of the cave of Mammon (*Faerie Queene* II, 7).

679. *erected*, 'upright,' in a double meaning—(1) of mind; (2) of bodily posture as explained in the following lines.

682. *trodden gold*, cf. Revelation xxi, 21, "And the street of the city was pure gold." So too the floor of the palace of Zeus was of gold (Homer, *Iliad*, IV, 2).

683. *aught . . . else* probably go together, though "else" might mean 'otherwise' ('which he might otherwise have enjoyed').

684. *vision beatific:* the sight of God himself, promised to the pure of heart (Matthew v, 8). The medieval theologians held the doctrine that the *visio beatifica* ("happy-making sight," as Milton translates the phrase in his poem *On Time*, 18) was the supreme joy of the saints.

686. *the centre* is often used to mean the earth, which was regarded as the centre of the world. *Cf.* Shakespeare, *Hamlet* II, ii, 157–159:

> . . . I will find
> Where truth is hid, though it were hid indeed
> Within the centre.

Troilus and Cressida I, iii, 85, "The heavens themselves the planets, and this centre."

But as the words "their mother earth" occur immediately after, "centre" here may mean 'the centre of the earth.' *Cf. Comus*, 381, "He that has light within his own clear breast/May sit i' the centre and enjoy bright day."

690. *admire*, 'wonder,' the Latin meaning. In 681 it has the usual meaning.

692. *precious bane* is probably an 'oxymoron'—a figure of speech in which an adjective seems to contradict its noun. It is a very effective device, often used by Milton.

It may be, however, that in this instance "precious" is used contemptuously.

694. *Babel:* probably the tower of Babel (Genesis xi, 4–9). It is sometimes explained as Babylon, but this seems less likely as we find "Babylon" further on (717).

694. *Memphian:* see note on 307.

"The works" are of course the pyramids.

695–699. There are again several 'double meanings' here. It is not easy to decide whether "strength and art" are nominatives, part of the subject of "are easily outdone," or genitives belonging to "monuments" and parallel to "fame"; and whether "in an hour" should go with "are easily outdone" or whether one should supply 'is performed' from "perform" in 699.

698–699. It was said that 366,000 men worked for twenty years to build the Great Pyramid.

700–717. It is not very easy to understand the exact methods of the angels, but it seems that they first smelted the ore in "many cells prepared," by means of fire from the burning lake, and then drew off the molten metal into trenches dug for the foundations ("a various mould"). From this the walls of the hall arose, by some magical means.

702. *Sluiced,* 'let in by sluices.'

702. *the lake:* the burning lake mentioned in 210.

703. *founded,* 'melted' as in a foundry.

704. *Severing,* 'separating.'

704. *bullion:* boiling metal in process of purification. The noun is used as an adjective here.

704. *dross,* 'scum' or 'impurities.'

708. *As in an organ.* This comparison would come readily to Milton's mind, since he was himself a good organist. He refers to the organ several times in his poems. In addition to playing the organ, Milton was a good all-round musician, as his father also was. There are many allusions to music in his works.

709. *sound-board:* a part of the mechanism of an organ, by means of which the air from the bellows is distributed to the various pipes which produce the notes.

709. *breathes,* 'sends air.'

711. *exhalation:* mist or vapour.

712. *symphonies:* music made by instruments, accompanying the voices.

713–716. The building resembled a Greek temple. It had *pilasters*—flat pillars set against the wall; *Doric pillars*—fluted columns with a simple capital or top; *architrave*—the main beam resting on the pillars; *frieze*—a decorative band above the architrave, sometimes with figures carved upon it; *and cornice*—a projecting band below the roof.

716. *bossy,* 'in relief.' A 'boss' is the carved knob where ribs of vaulting cross one another.

717. *fretted,* ornamented with strips of gold dividing it into squares, a favourite form of ceiling decoration in Elizabethan buildings.

This passage is thought to have been suggested by the gorgeous scenery and mechanical devices used in the masques performed at the court of Charles I. There is a description of one of these (cited by Todd), which is very close to Milton's idea:

In the further part of the scene, the earth opened; and there rose up a richly adorned palace, seeming all of goldsmith's work, with porticos vaulted, on pilasters of rustic work; their bases and capitals of gold. Above these ran an architrave, frieze, and cornice of the same, the frieze enriched with jewels.

718. *Alcairo:* Cairo ('Kahira.' *Al* is the Arabic definite article), was built in the tenth century near the ancient Memphis, which it superseded as the capital of Egypt. Though using this late name, Milton evidently means Memphis.

720. *Belus:* (Baal). See note on 412.

720. *Serapis,* with the accent on the first syllable instead of on the second as is usual now. Serapis was a late addition to the gods of Egypt, his worship having been introduced by Ptolemy I. There was a famous temple in his honour at Alexandria, and also one at Memphis.

723. *Stood fixed her stately highth* probably combines two ideas—(1) 'stood fixed'; (2) 'stood her stately highth' ('stood its full height').

724. *folds:* 'leaves' of folding doors.

724. *discover,* 'display,' 'reveal.'

726 *ff.* There is irony here. The devils make their grandiose but really pitiful attempt to mimic the universe. The vaulted roof corresponds to the vault of the sky and the cressets to its stars.

728. *cressets:* iron baskets to hold fire and serve as torches.

729. *naphtha* is a substance resembling petroleum; asphalt is its solid form.

730. *hasty,* 'hurrying,' 'eager.'

732. *the architect.* Many editors assume that "the architect," later called "Mulciber" (740), is the same as Mammon. But there seems no reason to suppose this. Their spheres of activity are different, Mammon representing riches, while Mulciber is a craftsman. The long description of "the architect" or "Mulciber" comes very late if it really applies to Mammon, who has already been described in 679 *ff.*

735. *supreme* has the accent on the first syllable, as in II, 210, "Our supreme foe in time much may remit."

737. *Each in his hierarchy,* 'each according to his angelic rank.' On the hierarchies see Introduction (p. 31).

739. *Ausonian land:* Italy, the land of the Ausones, an ancient people who inhabited the country before the coming of the Romans.

740. *Mulciber* is supposed to mean 'the softener,' *i.e.,* he who softens or melts metals, the smith. This was one of the names of Vulcan.

740–746. The story is told in Homer (*Iliad* I, 591–594) by Hephaestus himself, very briefly and in a rather humorous way. Milton elaborates it, stressing the length of time by dividing it into several parts of a day, finally making it "a summer's day," *i.e.*, a long one.

741. *angry Jove.* He was angry because Hephaestus (Vulcan) had supported his mother Juno in a quarrel between them.

742. *the crystal battlements.* Milton transfers to the palace of Jove the "crystal battlements" which properly belong to Heaven. *Cf.* VI, 859–860, "the bounds and crystal wall of Heaven."

745. *zenith:* the part of the sky immediately overhead.

746. *Lemnos:* an island in the northern part of the Aegean Sea.

747. *Erring.* The legend is incorrect, Milton says, because Mulciber (Vulcan) is really the devil-architect, who had fallen "long before."

747. *rout,* 'troop,' 'company.'

750. *engines,* 'inventions,' 'contrivances.' It is the same word as 'ingenious.'

752. *haralds* ('heralds'). An Italian form; *cf.* "sovran" in the next line and in 246 (see note) and "soldan" (765). Milton evidently had a liking for the Italian forms.

753. *awful,* ('full of awe'), 'impressive'; *cf.* 'respectful.'

756. *Pandemonium:* the home of all the demons, as the Pantheon is the temple of all the gods (from the Greek word *pan,* 'all'). The word has of course not yet got the meaning we now attach to 'pandemonium.' Milton invented the word.

758. *squared regiment,* 'squadron.' *Cf.* 356, "from every squadron and each band."

759. *By place or choice, i.e.,* because of their own rank or by election.

760. *With . . . attended,* 'attended by.'

761. *access,* 'entrance.' The accent is on the second syllable.

761. *the gates . . . hall.* The verb, "thick swarmed," does not come till after the parenthesis.

763-766. Here Milton again refers to the old stories of chivalry and to the single combats, serious or sportive, of the Christian and the Saracen ('panim' or 'paynin,' meaning 'pagan') champions. To give greater vividness, he uses some of the technical terms belonging to these stories—"champions" and "career," as well as the forms "Soldan" for "Sultan" and "Panim" for 'pagan,' which were usual in them.

763. *Though like a covered field.* The hall was as big as a tournament ground.

763. *covered field* is usually explained as a reference to, or translation of, the French expression *champ clos*, meaning a tournament-ground or 'lists'; this however was not covered but merely enclosed.

764. *wont*, 'were wont.' *Cf.* 332, "as when men wont to watch."

764. *at the Soldan's chair*, *i.e.*, in his very presence.

766. *mortal combat, or career with lance.* These were the two kinds of duel, the first in earnest, when the death or mortal injury of one of the combatants was the end, the second a sport or trial of skill, in which blunt weapons were used and no serious harm befell either of the combatants.

766. *career* is a technical term, meaning a short but swift gallop.

768. A wonderful line, the sound of the words most vividly suggesting the sound made by the angels' wings.

768-775. Milton here makes use of a comparison frequently occurring in poetry from Homer and Virgil onwards. The image of a bee-hive as a social or political allegory was a Renaissance commonplace; *cf.* Shakespeare, *Henry V*, I, ii, 187 *ff.* A swarm of bees is indeed a very natural image for a crowd of men, but Milton introduces a further comparison by making the bees discuss their affairs, as the angels are about to do.

This is the fifth simile which Milton has used to typify the numbers of the fallen angels (leaves in 302, sedge in 304, locusts in 340–343, a barbarian horde in 351–355). Here the simile illustrates not only the numbers of the angels but also the sound of their wings and the closeness with which they were crowded.

769. *Taurus:* the Bull, one of the signs of the Zodiac. In April and May the sun appears to pass through that part of the sky dominated by the constellation of Taurus.

769. *rides.* The sun "rides" in his chariot.

773. *suburb.* The plank is the board on which the bees alight, just outside the hive, hence a kind of 'suburb.'

773. *straw-built:* a 'skep' or hive made of twisted straw.

774. *New rubbed with balm:* to attract the bees by its sweet scent.

774. *expatiate,* 'walk about,' the Latin meaning.

774. *confer,* 'confer on,' 'discuss.' *Cf.* 661, "think submission."

776. *straitened,* 'crowded.'

777–780. Milton has already told us that the angels could alter their size at will, in 428–430.

778. *Earth's giant sons. Cf.* 197–199 and notes.

780. *that,* i.e., 'the famous'; *cf. Nativity Ode,* 199, "that twice-battered god of Palestine."

780. *pygmaean race, cf.* 575–576 and note.

781. *the Indian mount:* the western Himalayas.

781–784. We are reminded of Bottom's adventure in Shakespeare's *Midsummer Night's Dream.*

785. *arbitress* is generally explained as meaning 'witness.' But Milton nowhere else uses 'arbiter,' 'arbitrate,' etc., in this sense, but always as meaning 'judge.' So here it seems probable that the moon is presiding over the revels of the fairies.

785. *nearer to the earth.* Witches were supposed to be able to draw the moon down to the earth by their spells, an

explanation that is sometimes put forward here. But fairies do not appear to have this power, and it seems simpler to suppose that the moon has come closer in order to see their revels better.

786. *her pale course.* Strictly speaking, it is of course the moon herself who is pale.

790. *at large,* the opposite of "straitened" (776)—they had ample room.

795. *close,* 'secret.'

795. *recess,* 'retirement.'

795. *conclave:* a private apartment, especially one used by the cardinals when electing a pope, and hence usually the assembly of cardinals itself. Milton here uses the word for the assembly of devils, in sarcastic allusion to its ordinary meaning.

797. *Frequent,* here in its Latin meaning of 'crowded,' 'numerous.'

797. *full,* as we say 'a full house.'

798. *summons read,* 'the reading of the summons.' A Latin way of speaking. See note on 573.

798. *consult,* 'consultation.' The accent is on the second syllable.

Book II

1 *ff*. For the significance of the infernal council see Introduction, p. 38.

1-4. In Book V, 756–759 there is a description of Satan's palace in Heaven, before his fall:

> . . . his royal seat
> High on a hill, far blazing, as a mount
> Raised on a mount, with pyramids and towers,
> From diamond quarries hewn and rocks of gold.

2. *Ormus* (or Hormuz) was a city on an island at the mouth of the Persian Gulf. In the sixteenth and seventeenth centuries it was an important centre of trade between Europe and the East, particularly in jewels of all sorts, and was proverbial for its wealth. It is often mentioned in travel books of the period, but is now in ruins.

3. *Or where*, *i.e.*, 'or of those places where.'

4. *Showers on her kings . . . gold.* This is said to have been
5. customary at great ceremonies in the East.

merit. See note on I, 98.

6. *from*, 'after.'

In I, 126 Satan is "racked with deep despair," in spite of his boastful words. But gradually he grows more and more confident, till in I, 524 his followers "found their chief/Not in despair." When he reviews his forces "his heart/Distends with pride" and in his speech to them (I, 622–662) he is completely confident of ultimate success. Now he is "high uplifted beyond hope."

9. *success*, in its old meaning of 'result,' 'issue,' 'course of events' whether good or bad. *Cf.* 122–123:

> . . . seem to cast
> Ominous conjecture on the whole success.

Lines 11–416. *The debate in Pandemonium.*

It had been pointed out by Newton that the demons wander from the point in the course of the discussion, as often happens in human debates. In his first speech to his assembled followers Satan had insisted that submission was out of the question, and that there was no alternative to war, the only question being whether it should be open or "understood." This decision was greeted with enthusiasm by the rest (I, 660–669). Later, in the council in Pandemonium, he took the same line, putting forward as the subject for discussion "Whether of open war, or covert guile." (II, 35–42.) Moloch opens the debate on these lines, declaring his own opinion—"My sentence is for open war" (51). Belial follows, at first ostensibly keeping to the point— "I should be much for open war . . ." (119), but gradually, carried away by his own eloquence, he goes behind the motion and says, "War therefore, open or concealed, alike/My voice dissuades." (187–188.) Mammon follows him on this track and speaks as if the question were 'war or no war,' instead of 'open or concealed,' and he ends by "dismissing quite/All thoughts of war" (282–283). And his speech is hailed with considerable enthusiasm though the policy advocated was exactly the opposite of Satan's. The demons are as easily swayed by clever oratory as any human audience. The situation is saved by Beelzebub. Obviously it would not have suited either him or Satan if the demons had relapsed into acquiescence in the situation, for all hope of their own dominance would have been lost. Beelzebub, no less than the previous speakers, is a clever orator, and also quick to read the minds of his hearers. He shows them that the sort of peace they desire is unattainable, but he does not urge a direct attack on heaven, realizing that they were terrified of any such attempt (292–295 and 341–345). He settles the matter by a concrete proposal of definite action, which is at once accepted and welcomed. He continues his speech at once, without giving his audience a chance to change their minds as they had done after Mammon's speech. Then he cleverly leads up to the necessity of choosing a leader (402–416), pretending that this is an open question, but doubtless having arranged beforehand with Satan (as part of their plot in 379–380) that this should be Satan himself. Satan loses no time in making his offer (430–466).

The whole debate reflects Milton's familiarity with political discussion in all its aspects, and also with some characteristic types of politician, shown in the vivid portraits of the chief speakers among the fallen angels.

Another interesting point concerning this debate is the parallel between it and the discussion in Heaven about the fate of mankind, after the fall of Adam and Eve (III, 80–371). Having declared that though by his grace he will pardon them, yet Justice must be satisfied, and that man must die unless "Some other able, and as willing, pay/The rigid satisfaction, death for death" (III, 211–212), God asks which of the angels will thus redeem man:

> He asked, but all the heavenly quire stood mute,
> And silence was in Heaven: on man's behalf
> Patron or Intercessor none appeared,
> Much less that durst upon his own head draw
> The deadly forfeiture and ransom set.
>
> (III, 218–221)

Compare this with II, 417–434.

Christ then offers to undertake the task, an errand of love, as Satan's is an errand of hate.

The angels thereupon raise a joyful shout, then "lowly reverent/Towards either throne they bow" (III, 349–350). So in Hell after Satan's offer the devils rise with a noise like thunder, and then

> Towards him they bend
> With awful reverence prone; and as a god
> Extol him equal to the Highest in Heaven.
>
> (II, 477–479.)

11. *Powers and Dominions*. See Introduction, p. 31.

11. *deities of Heaven*. The rebel angels claimed to be themselves divine. So in VI, 156 Satan speaks of them as

> A third part of the Gods, in synod met
> Their deities to assert, who while they feel
> Vigour divine within them can allow
> Omnipotence to none.

12. *For, i.e.,* 'I call you deities of Heaven because . . .'
    12–17 are parenthetic.

12. *her*, where we should say 'its.' See note on I, 254.

14. *I give not Heaven for lost*, 'I do not regard Heaven as lost.'

15. *Virtues:* another order of angels, here applied to all the fallen ones.

16. *than from no fall*, 'than if they had never fallen.'

17. *trust themselves to fear no second fate*, 'have such confidence in themselves that they do not fear a second defeat.'

18–24. This complicated but effectively rhetorical sentence is like a Latin one in its general structure and also in details. There is first of all the emphatic position of "me" at the very beginning, the verb governing it not coming till nearly the end—"established" (23). The subject, "this loss," also comes very late. Between these comes a series of clauses with "did create" as verb.

Satan gives five reasons for his position of supremacy —(1) "just right," his former high rank in Heaven giving him a strong claim; (2) "the fixed laws of Heaven": *i.e.*, fate; (3) "free choice" of the other angels; (4) his pre-eminence both in planning and in actual fighting; (5) and most important, their defeat has put him in a position secure, free from envy, and willingly given by his companions. He then elaborates the idea of freedom from envy.

20–21. *Cf.* Satan's first speech to his assembled followers, I, 635–637.

24. *happier*, 'more fortunate' ('hap' = 'chance,' 'fortune').

25. *dignity*, 'worth,' another Latin meaning.

27. *whom*, 'him whom.'

28. *the Thunderer*. An epithet of Jupiter, here transferred to God. But there is a scornful tone in it, as before when Satan says "he with his thunder" (I, 93) and "he/ Whom thunder hath made greater" (I, 258).

29. *Your bulwark*, 'as your bulwark.'

33. *none*, *i.e.*, 'there is none.'

39–40. *Surer . . . assured*. There is here a double 'pun,' if one can call it so (surer—assured, prosper—prosperity). For another instance of a pun see I, 642 and note.

41. *open war or covert guile*. Satan had already given his opinion, in his former speech to his followers (I, 645-647).

> . . . our better part remains
> To work in close design, by fraud or guile,
> What force effected not.

43. *Moloch*. See note on I, 392.

His speech is in accord with his character—fierce and violent. Milton first gives a brief summary of it in his own words as narrator, and then lets Moloch speak for himself and elaborate the argument in detail. Thus 46-47 is elaborated in 60-70, and 47-48 in 92-98.

48. *Cared not, sc.* 'he.'

48. *with that care lost*, 'with the loss of that care.' (Latin construction.)

50. *recked*, 'cared.' Though we have lost the verb 'to reck,' we still use the adjective 'reckless.'

50. *thereafter*, probably means 'accordingly.'

51. *sentence*, 'opinion' or 'vote,' the meaning of the Latin *sententia. Cf.* 291, "his sentence pleased."

52. *inexpert*, 'inexperienced.'

56. *sit lingering*, contrasted with "sit contriving" (54).

57. *Heaven's fugitives*, 'fugitives from Heaven.'

59. *The prison of his tyranny.* (1) *of* here means 'assigned by.' (2) *his.* Moloch, like Satan, will not name God. But the word "his" is extremely emphatic. (3) *tyranny.* See note on I, 124.

60. *By our delay*, 'because we delay to attack him.'

61. *all at once*, 'all of us, immediately.'

63. *our tortures:* 'the instruments of our torture'—"Hell flames and fury."

63. *horrid*, 'bristling,' (*cf.* I, 563, "a horrid front"), and probably at the same time 'terrifying.'

65. *his almighty engine:* thunder. On "engine" see note on I, 750.

66. *Infernal*, coming from Hell, as contrasted with God's own [heavenly] thunder.

66. *for*, 'instead of.'

67. *Black fire:* the flames of Hell, which gave no light. *Cf.* I, 62–63:

> . . . from those flames
> No light, but darkness visible.

(See **note** on that passage.)

67. *equal, i.e.,* to that of their enemies.

69. *Mixed with*, 'filled with.'

69. *Tartarean.* Tartarus was the classical equivalent of Hell. Here we find Milton intermingling classical and biblical

ideas, as he often does, both being equally familiar to him. *Cf.* I, 239, "the Stygian flood."

69. *strange fire*: the "Black fire" of l. 67, not seen in Heaven before. But the words 'strange fire' occur in the Bible (Leviticus x, 1), which may have suggested them to Milton.

70. *His own invented torments.* God would be conquered by the very thing he had himself devised.

70 *ff.* Moloch proceeds to put forward and to refute (to his own satisfaction) the arguments which might be advanced against his proposal of war. These are (1) the difficulty of ascending from Hell to Heaven. But ascent is natural to angels (70–81). (2) If they do not succeed, they will be worse off than they are now. But nothing could be worse than their present situation. Any change for the worse would mean annihilation, which would itself be preferable to what they now endure (82–101). (3) And even if not fully successful, they can at least cause constant trouble (101–105).

72. *upright wing*, 'upward flight.'

73. *such, i.e.*, those who hold this.

73. *sleepy*, 'causing sleep.' So also "forgetful," 'causing forgetfulness.'

73. *drench*, 'draught,' 'drink,' still used in the restricted sense of a dose of medicine for a horse.

75–81. Satan had already spoken of this upward movement (I, 631–634).

75. *our proper motion*, 'the motion proper (*i.e.*, natural) to us.'

77. *adverse*, 'contrary to our nature.' Opposed to "proper."

77. *Who but felt*, 'Who was there who did not feel?"

79. *insulting*, 'attacking.'

82. *The event is feared*, Moloch speaks for some imagined objector.

82. *event*, 'result.' *Cf.* I, 624.

83. *Our stronger*, 'one stronger than we,' or 'our superior.'

87. *deep* here must be the pit of Hell, not Chaos as usually meant.

88. *unextinguishable.* Notice how this long, heavy word, coming among so many short ones, gives the idea of the duration and strength of the fire.

89. *exercise*, 'torment.'

90. *vassals.* The word now suggests feudalism, but Milton uses it as merely 'servants,' or 'slaves.' *Cf.* 251–252, "our state/Of splendid vassalage."

92. *Calls* in the singular, as the "scourge" and the "torturing hour" are parts of one idea, punishment. *Cf.* I, 139, "the mind and spirit remains."

92. *penance*, 'punishment.'

92. *More destroyed*, 'if we were more destroyed.'

93. *abolished*, 'annihilated,' 'destroyed.'

94. *What doubt we?* 'Why do we hesitate?' For 'what' = 'why.' *Cf.* 329, "What sit we then projecting peace or war?"

95. *to the highth*, 'to the utmost.' On the form of the word see note on I, 24.

97. *essential*, adjective, for the noun 'essence.' "This essential" is the "essence pure" of I, 425, and the "empyreal substance" of I, 117. Satan was sure that it could never be destroyed (I, 116–117) and so was Beelzebub (I, 138–140). Moloch is undecided. See note on I, 117.

97. *happier far . . . being.* To cease to exist is far better than to live for ever in misery.

100–101. *we are . . . nothing*, 'We are in the worst state possible short of annihilation.'

101. *proof*, 'experience.' Satan had made this point too in his speech to Beelzebub—especially I, 103–105 and 113–114.

104. *fatal*, 'established by fate.' Beelzebub had stated the three alternatives whether God's rule is "upheld by

strength, or chance, or fate," without deciding between them. (I, 133.)

105. *revenge:* Satan's own motive. (I, 107.)

106. *denounced,* 'proclaimed,' 'threatened.'

109 *ff.* Belial, like Moloch, speaks in character, advocating a policy of non-resistance and hoping (on no very good grounds) that things will get better and that he and his followers will live fairly comfortably in the end. His eloquence however somewhat disguises the "ignoble ease and peaceful sloth" on which his proposals are founded.

While all the speeches are more or less formally worked out, Belial's is the most noticeable for its rhetorical devices and verbal skill. It may be worth examining a small part of his speech as an example of this; lines 160–185 give much in small compass:

(1) One word or idea running like a guiding thread through the argument, *e.g.*—

163 What can we suffer worse? Is this then worst?
169 That sure was worse.
186 This would be worse.

(2) Repeated questions, introduced by the same word—

166 What when ... ?
170 What if ... ?
174 What if ... ?

(3) Emphasis produced by words of similar meaning, generally in groups of three—

160–161 decreed,/Reserved, and destined to eternal woe.

or introduced by the same word or syllable—

164 Thus sitting, thus consulting, thus in arms.
185 Unrespited, unpitied, unreprieved.

(In the last two examples the emphasis is increased by the omission of any word of connexion.)

(4) Repetition of a phrase with slight alteration—

162–163 what can we suffer more? / What can we suffer worse?

These and other rhetorical devices are frequent throughout Belial's speech.

109. *Belial.* See I, 490–500 and note.

109. *act*, 'action,' *i.e.*, words and behaviour.

109. *humane*, 'polished,' 'cultured.'

110. *A fairer person* is the object, not the subject, of "lost."

111. *dignity*, 'high rank.'

113. *manna, i.e.*, words sweet as manna (or honey). (Exodus xvi, 31.)

113–114. *could make . . . reason*—the very words of the charge brought against Socrates.

114. *to*, 'so as to.'

114. *dash*, 'overthrow,' 'confound.'

115. *for his thoughts were low* explains "all was false and hollow," the lines being a parenthesis.

119. Belial begins his speech by refuting Moloch's arguments.

121. *Main reason*, 'as the main reason.'

123. *Ominous conjecture*, 'foreboding and doubt.'

123. *success*, 'result,' as in 9. (See note.)

124. A neat compliment to Moloch, in keeping with Belial's character.

124. *fact of arms*, 'deeds' or 'feats' of arms—a literal translation of the French *'fait d'armes.'*

125–126. 'Lacking confidence in the policy he advocates and in recourse to war, in which he excels.'

126. *on despair.* Moloch had urged that nothing could be worse than their present case.

127. *utter dissolution.* Moloch had said that annihilation would be better than everlasting misery.

127. *scope*, 'object.'

128. *after some dire revenge.* A sneering way of speaking of

what was actually Moloch's aim and the purpose of his whole speech. Belial belittles this, and picks out for comment what Moloch had said in reply to possible objections, making light of his main point.

130. *render*, in the plural, because "watch" means 'watchmen.'

130. *access*, 'way of approach.' See note on I, 761.

131. *the bordering Deep:* the part of Chaos nearest to Heaven.

132. *obscure*, accented on the first syllable, as often in Shakespeare and Milton.

134–142. Belial destroys the hopes and plans expressed by Moloch in 60–70.

134. *Could we*, 'if we could.'

135. *all Hell should rise*, inversion for "should all Hell rise"; *i.e.*, 'if all Hell . . .'

139. *ethereal mould* is sometimes explained as the soil of Heaven, like "this ethereous mould on which we stand" (VI, 473). But it more probably refers to the substance of the angels (the "empyreal substance" of I, 117); "mould" means both shape and earth or the material of the body. So in the *Nativity Ode*, 138, "And leprous sin will melt from earthly mould"; *Arcades*, 72, "which none can hear/Of human mould." This meaning suits the context here better, since Moloch specially mentions his intended attack on the angels (66–68). This attack was to be by "black fire" (67); Belial says that the "ethereal mould" of the angels would "purge off the baser fire" (since it consists of heavenly fire).

141. *Her*, 'its' (the ethereal mould's).

141. *mischief*, 'pollution.'

142–146. This is not Belial's own opinion, but his version of Moloch's, (92–97). His own opinion is expressed in the following lines.

143. *flat*, 'absolute'; as we say 'a flat contradiction.'

147. *intellectual being:* referring to the kind of soul the

angels possessed. Plants, beasts, men, and angels had souls respectively vegetative, sensitive, rational, and intellectual.

149. *To perish rather*, 'and prefer to perish.'

152. *Let this be good*, 'granting for the sake of argument that this is good.'

153–154. *how he can/Is doubtful*. Belial is not quite sure whether the fallen angels are immortal; Satan had no doubts—"this empyreal substance cannot fail" (I, 117).

156 *Belike*, 'doubtless,' said ironically.

156. *impotence*, 'lack of self-control,' a frequent meaning of the Latin word.

156. *unaware*, 'accidentally.' Of course Belial is speaking ironically in applying these words to the Almighty.

157. *their wish*, according to Moloch.

159. *endless*, 'endlessly.'

159. *cease*, i.e., from carrying out the war.

159–163. Moloch's argument in 84–93, somewhat exaggerated.

160. *they who counsel war*. Belial clearly means Moloch, but puts it tactfully.

163–169. Belial's answer to Moloch's argument.

165. *What?* i.e., 'What was our state?'

165. *strook*, 'struck.' The form 'strook' seems always to have been used by Milton unless there was some special reason against it—*e.g.*, *Paradise Regained* III, 146, "Satan had not to answer, but stood struck," where 'stood strook' would have sounded absurd.

166. *afflicting*, probably in the literal sense of 'striking down'; *cf.* I, 186, "our afflicted powers."

168–169. A reference to their situation described in I, 48, 51–53, 311–313.

170. *the breath*, sc. of God's anger. Perhaps a reminiscence of Isaiah xxx, 33, "The breath of the Lord, like a stream of brimstone, doth kindle it" (of Tophet).

173. *intermitted, i.e.*, which had ceased for a time. Satan had noted that God had ceased to pursue and attack the fallen angels. (I, 169–177.)

174. *His red right hand*, a phrase used by Horace (*Odes* I, 2, 2–3) of Jove threatening to destroy Rome. By its use Belial insinuates that God is a tyrant like Jove.

175. *Her:* Hell's, like "her cataracts," in the next line. Here again we should say 'its.'

175. *firmament:* the vault covering Hell. *Cf.* I, 298, "vaulted with fire."

176. *cataracts*, 'torrents,' like the "floods and whirlwinds of tempestuous fire" of I, 77.

177. *Impendent*, 'hanging over us' (the literal sense).

179. *glorious* is of course ironical.

180–181. *Caught . . . transfixed*, as Satan had expected (I, 325–329). The idea may come from Virgil's description of the death of Ajax (*Aeneid* I, 44–45).

181. *the sport and prey.* An idea expressed by many great poets—Aeschylus, Virgil, Horace, Dryden, and others.

182. *racking* probably means 'tormenting'; *cf.* I, 126, "racked with deep despair"; but it may mean 'driving them along,' like clouds before the wind. ('cloud-rack.')

183. Repeats "In adamantine chains and penal fire" of I, 48. The "boiling ocean" is the "fiery gulf" of I, 52 and "fiery waves" of I, 184.

184. *converse* does not mean 'talk to' but 'live with,' the meaning of the Latin word *conversor*.

185. *Unrespited, unpitied, unreprieved.* The use of a series of words (usually three) with the same (negative) beginning is a frequent and effective poetical device, from the Greek writers onwards. Scott's "unwept, unhonoured and unsung" (*Lay of the Last Minstrel*) is a well-known example. Milton uses it in prose also, *e.g.*, (a bishop) "undiocesed, unrevenued, unlorded."

186. *hopeless* really applies to "ages," (or even to the victims, not mentioned). The meaning is of course 'ages to which no end can be hoped.'

186. *this would be worse*. With these four short, emphatic words Belial concludes his argument against Moloch. He now goes on to give his own opinion.

187. *War . . . open or concealed*. Satan had said, "War, then, war/Open or understood, must be resolved" (I, 661–662).

188. *voice*, 'opinion.'

188. *what can*, 'What power have . . . ?'—the meaning of the Latin *possum*.

189–193. Belial recognizes the omniscience as well as the omnipotence of God, as none of the others do, not even Satan himself.

190–191. *Cf*. Psalm 2, 4, "He that sitteth in the heavens shall laugh: the Lord shall have them in derision"—a very appropriate reference since the devils are the exact counterpart of the "kings of the earth" and the "rulers" at whom the Lord laughs.

191. *motions*, 'plans,' 'proposals,' as we say 'The motion before the meeting is . . .'

194–196. *Shall we . . . torments*. Belial mentions a possible objection, in order to forestall it.

197. *fate*. Belial identifies fate with the will of God, as God himself says (VII, 173) "What I will is fate." Satan (in I, 115–116) speaks as if fate were above God.

199. *To suffer, as to do, cf*. I, 157–158 and note.

200. *nor the law unjust*. Belial alone acknowledges the justice of God's decree.

201. *this was at first resolved*. "Was" is an over-statement for 'must have been'—'We must have made up our minds to this at the outset, since we were contending against so great a foe and were uncertain what would happen.'

203. *fall*, 'befall,' 'happen.'

204. *at the spear*, i.e., in battle.

210. *supreme*, accented on the first syllable; cf. I, 735, " the supreme King."

210. *remit*, 'slacken,' 'relax.'

211. *thus far removed*, 'since we are so far away.' *Cf.* I, 73–74:

> As far removed from God and light of heaven
> As from the centre thrice to the utmost pole.

212. *mind*, 'remember,' 'think of,' as still in some English dialects.

212. *not offending*, 'if we do not offend him.'

212–213. *satisfied . . . punished*, 'satisfied with the punishment already inflicted.' The idea is like that expressed by Satan in I, 179.

214. *if his breath stir not their flames*, as it had kindled them (see 170).

215–216. Belial thinks that the fallen angels will be able to overcome the flames of hell by the greater purity of their "essence," just as those in heaven could (139–142).

215–216. *Our purer essence: cf.* the "empyreal substance" (I, 117) and "heavenly essences" (I, 138), where see notes.

216. *vapour* may mean either 'fumes' or 'heat.'

216. *inured*, 'growing accustomed to it.'

217. *to the place conformed*, 'adapted to our surroundings.'

218. *temper*. According to medieval physiology, the body contained four 'humours,' or fluids, which being mixed in different proportions ('tempered'; see note on I, 285) produced different mental and physical characters or dispositions. Hence our word 'temperament.'

219. *Familiar*, 'as an accustomed thing,' 'as a matter of course.'

220. *light* is sometimes explained as an adjective (balancing "mild"). It is more likely to be a noun, "light" as

opposed to "darkness," the most natural meaning. And the contradiction of terms ('oxymoron') is characteristic of Milton's style. The idea is that the darkness of Hell may in time seem to them to be light.

223. *waiting*, sc. 'for.'

224. *For happy . . . worst*, 'regarded as happiness, certainly bad; but if regarded as bad, not the worst.' Belial means that if they compare their present lot with their former happiness in Heaven, it is a miserable one; but if they compare it with what it might be after another war, it is not the worst possible.

226. Belial has much in common with Comus; one likeness is suggested here, in his use of "words clothed in reason's garb" just as (according to the Lady) Comus used "false rules pranked in reason's garb." (*Comus*, 759.) This is more than just a verbal resemblance.

228. *Mammon*. See I, 678 *ff*. and note.

229 *ff*. Mammon in his speech agrees with Belial in being opposed to war; but his policy is more active—instead of merely hoping to escape God's anger by acquiescence and inaction, Mammon wishes the fallen angels to create a new life for themselves by their own efforts in making the best possible use of their circumstances.

230. *We war*, 'we shall make war.'

231. *lost*, 'which we have lost.'

231–233. *then . . . strife*, *i.e.*, never.

232–233. *everlasting Fate . . . strife*. A double impossibility, since (1) "everlasting" Fate could never yield to "fickle" Chance, and (2) such a victory could only be made even to seem possible by the appointment of Chaos as judge; since Chance is one of the attendants of Chaos (965), Chaos would be a very biased judge.

It seems clear that the "strife" is between Fate and Chance, not, as has sometimes been suggested, between God and the fallen angels.

234. *The former:* "to disenthrone the King of Heaven." (229.)

234. *vain to hope,* 'which it is vain to hope for.'

234. *argues,* 'proves.'

235. *The latter:* "to regain/Our own right lost." (230–231.)

244. *breathes,* 'is redolent of.'

245. *Ambrosial,* 'heavenly,' 'immortal.' In classical mythology 'ambrosia' was the food of the gods.

249. *To whom, i.e.,* 'to him whom.'

249. *pursue,* 'seek,' 'try to regain.' The object of the verb is "our state of splendid vassalage" (251–252).

250. 'which it is impossible to obtain by force, and which would not be acceptable if obtained by the permission of God.'

251. *Unacceptable.* Scan 'unáccéptáble.'

252–257. Mammon here expresses a view close to that of Satan in I, 258–263.

We may note his particular kind of rhetoric, the use of adjectives and nouns of contradictory sense, *e.g.,* "splendid vassalage" (252), "servile pomp" (257).

253. *from our own, sc.* 'resources'; 'on our own account.'

254. *Live to ourselves,* 'live our own lives,' 'be our own masters.'

254. *recess,* 'retreat.'

258. *of,* 'out of.'

263–267. So for example on Mount Horeb (Exodus xix, 8, Deuteronomy iv, 11), and at the dedication of the Temple (II Chronicles v, 13, and vi, 1). There are many similar references in the Psalms and elsewhere in the Bible.

270–273. Mammon of course knows about the precious metals to be found in the earth; even when still in heaven his chief interest had been in such things (I, 680–683) and it was he who had directed the mining and smelting of precious metals for the building of Pandemonium

(I, 678, 688 *ff*) as well as teaching such things to mankind later (I, 684–688).

271. *Wants*, 'lacks.'

273. *Magnificence, i.e.*, magnificent works, especially perhaps buildings, of which Pandemonium is an example.

274–278. Mammon takes up Belial's idea, expressed in 217–220.

275. *elements*. In medieval lore the four 'elements'—fire, air, water, and earth—were each ruled by their own special 'daemons,' which were believed to be the same as the fallen angels. In *Paradise Regained* II, 122–124, Satan addresses the angels as

> Demonian spirits now, from the element
> Each of his reign, allotted, rightlier called
> Powers of fire, air, water and earth beneath.

276. *temper*. See note on 218.

278. *sensible*, 'sensation,' 'sense.'

280. *how* depends on "counsels"—'to consult how.'

281. *Compose*, 'settle,' 'arrange.'

281–282. *with regard . . . were*, 'taking into consideration our present (restricted) state, compared with what we once were.'

284–290. The applause of Mammon's audience is evidently a low, restrained murmur, different from the noisy applause with which they received Satan's rousing challenge to war in I, 663–669. Having heard the persuasive speeches of Belial and Mammon against war, their mood is now very different, and their eagerness for war has vanished. But they dare not express their feelings strongly, knowing that Satan will disapprove.

Milton must have known many descriptions of calm succeeding storm on a rocky coast in poetry and in old travel books, but here again he makes his description more telling by connecting it with human life, as represented by the "sea-faring men." We are reminded of the peasant's glimpse of fairies in I, 782–785, and the story of the sailors anchoring their boat to a whale (I, 203–207).

287. *cadence:* a 'falling' sound, as the winds die down.

287. *lull*, 'and which [*sc.* the winds] now lull.'

288. *o'erwatched*, 'tired out with being awake.'

289. *pinnace*, a small boat, often serving as a tender for a larger one.

291. *sentence. Cf.* 51 and note.

294. *thunder and the sword of Michael:* the two great weapons in the defence of Heaven. Thunder has already been mentioned several times, *e.g.*, I, 93, 258; II, 166. In the description of the battle in Heaven in Book VI, we hear of the immense power of Michael's sword, "from the armoury of God," which "felled squadrons at once" and wounded Satan himself.

(*Michael*, like *Raphael*, has three syllables.)

297. *policy*, 'statesmanship.'

297. *process*, accented on the second syllable.

298. *In emulation . . . Heaven.* This is a difficult phrase, perhaps best explained by taking "emulation" (rivalry) closely with "which might rise." We may paraphrase "which might in time arise to be the rival and opposite of Heaven." Hell is "opposite" in three ways: (1) being situated below Chaos while Heaven is above it, (2) contrary to Heaven in nature and purpose, (3) hostile.

299. *Beelzebub.* See I, 79–81 and note.

301. *Aspect*, accented on the second syllable, as it usually was in Milton's time.

302. *front*, 'forehead.'

303. *public care*, 'care for the public (the state).'

306. *Atlantean:* shoulders as strong as those of Atlas, a giant of Greek mythology who carried the sky upon his shoulders to prevent it from falling on to the earth.

308. *audience*, 'a hearing.'

309. *summer's noontide air*. Proverbially still and windless especially in southern countries, where every one rest, at mid-day.

312. *style*, 'title.' Newly-created peers are still gazetted 'by the names, styles, and titles of . . .'

313. *Princes of Hell* instead of "offspring of heaven."

315. *doubtless* is of course sarcastic.

321. *thus far removed*. Beelzebub is quoting Belial, who had suggested that God might forget about them, when they were "thus far removed" (211).

322. *the inevitable curb*, 'the restraint from which there is no escape.'

324. *highth or depth:* Heaven or Hell.

324. *first and last*. Revelation i, 11, "I am Alpha and Omega, the first and the last." So also Revelation xxi, 6, and xxii, 13.

327. *iron sceptre . . . golden*. Iron represents severity, gold mildness. So in *Lycidas* (110–111) Milton says of St Peter:

> Two massy keys he bore of metals twain,
> (The golden opes, the iron shuts amain).

The scriptural reference is to Psalm 2, 9, "Thou shalt break them with a rod of iron," and Revelation ii, 27, "He shall rule them with a rod of iron" (the latter having become proverbial). Milton uses the phrase again in V, 886–888 where Abdiel warns Satan that

> That golden sceptre which thou didst reject
> Is now an iron rod to bruise and break
> Thy disobedience.

329. *What* = why? *Cf.* 94, "What doubt we?"

330. *determined us*, 'decided our fate.'

332 *Voutsafed*. The spelling seems to represent Milton's pronunciation of this word, avoiding the unpleasing sound of 'vouchsafed.'

336. *to our power*, 'to the best of our ability,' 'as far as we can.'

337. *reluctance*, 'resistance,' 'struggle against,' the Latin meaning, much stronger than that now given to the word.

339. *reap his conquest*, 'reap the advantage of his conquest.'

341. *occasion*, 'opportunity.'

341. *want*, 'be lacking.' *Cf.* "nor did there want/Cornice or frieze" (I, 715–716).

345 *ff*. This rumour had already been referred to by Satan, I, 651–654.

346. *fame*, 'rumour,' 'report.'

347. *seat*, 'home.'

349–350. Psalm 8, 5, "Thou hast made him a little lower than the angels, and hast crowned him with glory and honour."

352. The rather strange idea of God swearing an oath occurs several times in the Bible—*e.g.*, Genesis xxii, 16, Hebrews vi, 17. The shaking of Heaven, however, comes from the classical epic, so that we have here another instance of Milton's fusing of classical and biblical traditions.

355. *inhabit*, 'dwell,' (intransitive as often in Milton's time).

355. *mould*, 'form,' *cf.* 139, "ethereal mould." (See note.)

356. *how endued*, 'endowed with what qualities.'

357. *how attempted*, 'how an attempt (attack) could best be made on them.'

358. *by force or subtlety*. A double question, whether by force or by subtlety? "Subtlety" being the eventual choice was suitably put into practice by the serpent, which was "more subtle than any beast of the field" (Genesis iii, 1).

359. *Arbitrator*, 'ruler.'

362. *their* is emphatic—the inhabitants of the earth.

365. *waste*, 'lay waste.'

367. *drive*, 'drive out.'

369. *with repenting hand*, *cf.* Genesis vi, 6, 7, "And it re
pented the Lord that he had made man on the earth
And the Lord said 'I will destroy man whom I hav
created'."

371–372. *his joy/In our confusion*, *i.e.*, joy caused to him b
our downfall. So in the next line the meaning is 'jo
caused to us by his disturbance.'

373. *disturbance* has much the same meaning as "confusion."

374. *partake with us*, 'share our lot.'

375. *original* here means 'originator,' *i.e.*, 'parent,' namel
Adam. For this meaning of the word *cf.* Shakespeare
Midsummer Night's Dream II, i, 117, "We are thei
parents and original."

376. *Advise*, 'consider.'

377. *or to sit*, 'or whether it is better to sit.'

378. *vain empires*. A sarcastic reference to that for whic
Mammon hoped (II, 252 *ff.*).

379–380. *first devised/By Satan*, in I, 650–656. Satan ha
indeed suggested the idea, but vaguely and as only on
of several possible schemes. Beelzebub (perhap
helped by Satan) puts forward a practicable plan fo
carrying it out. Satan thus makes use of the wel
known device of getting some one else to propose hi
plan, keeping in the background himself until th
crucial moment.

382. *confound*, 'ruin.'

383. *one root*: Adam.

385. *still*, 'constantly.' *Cf.* I, 68 note.

387. *States*, 'princes.'

391. *Synod* means any meeting or assembly, but is use
more particularly of ecclesiastical assemblies. So in
795 Milton calls the assembly of demons a "conclave.
See note there.

391–392. *like to what ye are . . . resolved*, 'made a great decision, in accordance with your own greatness.'

393. *in spite of fate.* Beelzebub is denying Belial's statement (197–198) "Since fate inevitable/Subdues us."

394. *seat*, 'home,' as in 347. Beelzebub of course means by this 'Heaven.'

395. *those bright confines:* a region bordering on Heaven and lit by its light; or perhaps the crystal walls of Heaven themselves.

395. *neighbouring*, conveniently close to Heaven.

396. *excursion*, 'sortie,' like the "first eruption" mentioned by Satan (I, 656).

396. *chance.* 'To' is understood before "re-enter."

399. *Secure*, 'without anxiety,' the Latin meaning of the word.

399. *brightening*, 'which makes bright.'

399. *orient.* See note on I, 546.

400. *Purge off*, suggesting that darkness is a sort of pollution.

400. *this gloom:* the darkness of Chaos.

401. *the scar*, like the "deep scars of thunder" on Satan's face. (I, 601.)

401. *corrosive*, 'gnawing,' 'eating into.'

402. *her*, 'its.'

404. *Sufficient*, 'fit for an office or enterprise.' In *Othello* I, iii, 225, the Duke says that there is in Cyprus a commander "of most allowed sufficiency."

404. *tempt*, 'attempt,' 'venture into.'

405. *Abyss:* Chaos.

406. *palpable obscure*, 'darkness which may be felt,' like that which was sent to plague the Egyptians, Exodus x, 21.

407. *uncouth*, 'unknown,' 'strange.' The accent is on the first syllable, as in 827.

408. *indefatigable*, 'never wearied.'

409. *abrupt*, 'chasm,' 'gap,' between Heaven and Hell (Chaos).

409. *arrive*, 'arrive at,' 'reach,' as often at this time.

410. *The happy isle:* the earth, which is a sort of island in Chaos.

411. *evasion*, 'means of escape.'

412. *senteries*, 'sentries.'

412. *stations*, 'guards,' the Latin meaning.

412–413. This seems to contradict what Beelzebub had previously said himself in his first speech (360–362). But then he was trying to encourage the demons to war and minimizing the difficulties; now he is making the most of the difficulties, in order to discourage any who might offer to attempt the task of making their way to the earth, and thus to leave it open for Satan.

413. *had need*, 'would have need of.'

414. *no less*, *sc.* 'have need of.' 'We need to be as cautious in choosing our emissary as he will need to be on his journey.' *We* is emphatic.

415. *choice*, 'careful judgment.'

415. *suffrage*, vote to select the emissary.

418. *suspense*, 'in suspense.'

418. *appeared*, 'should appear.'

419. *second*, 'speak in favour of his proposal.'

423. *Astonished*, 'aghast'—a much stronger expression than it is now. *Cf.* I, 266 note.

423. *prime*, 'foremost,' 'chief.' *Cf.* I, 506.

425. *hardy*, 'bold.'

425. *proffer*, 'offer his service.'

429. *unmoved* by the prospect of danger, which had so perturbed the rest.

431. *demur*, 'hesitation.'

432. *though undismayed*. He flatters them, for they were dismayed (421–423).

432–433. *Long is the way . . . light*. It being no longer necessary to encourage his followers to make open war, Satan

contradicts what Moloch had said (75–81). He stresses
the difficulties of the task, as Beelzebub had done, to
prevent any of the rest from volunteering. (Notice the
effect of slow and difficult movement given by the use
of words of one syllable, and of the repetition of *h* and
l sounds.)

432 *ff.* In this passage Milton doubtless had in mind Virgil's description of Aeneas' descent into Hell (*Aeneid*,
VI) especially the Sibyl's warning of the difficulty of
return. There are other similarities of detail: the "convex of fire . . . immures us round/Ninefold"—as in
Virgil the river Styx imprisons the dwellers in Hell
with ninefold winding; and in Virgil the gates of Hell
have columns of solid adamant, like Milton's "gates of
burning adamant."

434. *convex of fire:* the vault of fire which covered Hell,
"vaulted with fire" (I, 298). *Cf.* "Hell's concave" (I,
542), "the fiery concave" (II, 635). There is no need to
insist on the distinction between 'convex' and 'concave.' We are dealing with poetry, not geometry.

435. *outrageous to devour,* 'eager to consume us.'

435. *immures us round,* 'walls us in.'

438. *These passed,* 'when these have been passed.' An 'absolute' construction.

438. *the void profound:* Chaos.

439. *unessential,* 'insubstantial'—without real substance.

441. *abortive.* It is impossible to give any precise equivalent
for this word, as it includes several meanings, as so often
in Milton's writing. There is the idea of 'prematurely
born,' hence 'shapeless,' 'formless,' 'monstrous'; or
the active sense of 'causing premature birth' (*cf.* "forgetful," 74), hence 'life-destroying,' 'deadly.' Compare
624–625:

> Where all life dies, death lives, and Nature breeds.
> Perverse, all monstrous, all prodigious things.

442–444. 'If he escapes from this place into some other world or unknown region, what awaits him but at best unknown dangers and the difficulty of escape?'

443. *remains him*, 'remains for him,' another Latin use.

447–448. *if aught . . . danger*, 'if any proposal . . . involving difficulty or danger.'

448. *moment*, 'importance.' 'Momentous' still has the same meaning.

450. *Me.* Very emphatic. (1) by its position at the beginning of the line, (2) by its shortness, (3) by the run of the verse in "Mé from attémpting."

451. *royalties*, 'royal powers.'

451. *and not refuse*, 'instead of refusing.'

452. *Refusing*, 'if I refuse.'

453–456. *due alike . . . sits.* Since hazard and honour are equally due to him who reigns, and the more highly he is honoured, the more hazard he must accept.

457–462. This is very like Mammon's plan (260–262), but instead of being a chief object is only a temporary expedient.

457. *intend*, 'attend to,' 'consider.'

461. *deceive*, 'beguile.'

461. *slack*, 'slacken.'

462. *mansion*, 'dwelling-place.' *Cf.* I, 268 and note.

462. *intermit*, 'omit.'

464. *coasts*, 'regions.' *Cf.* I, 340.

466. *None shall partake with me.* The abruptness and peremptoriness of Satan's closing remark is emphasized by its breaking off in the middle of a line, the short, simple words, and the stress thrown upon "me."

467. *prevented*, 'forestalled.' 'To prevent' originally meant 'to go, or arrive, before,' whether with a good or a bad purpose. So in the *Nativity Ode*, 24, the Muse is bidden to "prevent" the wise men going to Bethlehem, *i.e.*

arrive there before them. Now the subsidiary idea of 'hindering' has become the chief one.

46 8. *from*, 'by.'

468. *his*. Emphatic because of the metre, contrasted with "others."

468. *raised*, 'encouraged,' as in 521.

470. *Certain to be refused* may mean 'since they were sure their offer would be refused'; but more probably "refused" belongs with "others," as it must in the next line—"that they would not be accepted."

470. *erst*, 'previously.'

471. *opinion*, 'public opinion'—in the view of the other devils.

471. *stand*, 'hold the position of,' 'be regarded as.'

475. *Forbidding:* "this enterprise/None shall partake with me." (465–466.)

478. *awful*, 'full of awe.' *Cf.* 'respectful.'

480. *praised*, 'strongly approved.'

482. *neither* looks forward to the next sentence—'bad men should not boast, for neither . . .'

483. *lest*. One must understand some such words as 'I say this' (to prevent bad men from boasting).

483. *boast*, 'boast of.'

484. *specious*, 'noble in appearance,' 'on the surface.'

484. *glory*, 'love of glory.'

485. *close*, 'secret,' usually with a suggestion of evil, 'crafty.'

485. *varnished o'er* carries on the idea of "specious."

486. *their doubtful consultations dark* refers to the earlier part of the long debate, ended by their agreement and pride in their leader.

488–495. This wonderful simile exactly fits the course of the debate and its ending, and at the same time it marks the subject off clearly and forms a sort of interlude before the beginning of the next episode. Apart from the uncommon use of a few words, the language is simple and straightforward, without rhetorical devices or difficulties of any kind, quickly giving us a vivid and true picture.

489. *while the north wind sleeps.* When it blows, the sky is generally clear.

490. *element:* the sky.

491. *Scowls.* A very effective use of the word in a transitive sense ('scowls as it drives').

491. *lantskip.* The form of the word always used by Milton. We now say 'landscape.'

492. *chance,* 'if it chances that.' *Cf. Comus,* 507, "How chance she is not in your company?" ('how does it happen that . . . ?').

494. *bleating* is any animal noise; *cf.* I, 489.

495. *that,* 'so that.'

495. *rings.* A singular verb with two subjects ("hill and valley"), which, however, form a single idea.

496–505. Milton is evidently speaking with deep personal feeling of the discords and civil wars which filled so much of his lifetime.

497. *Firm concord,* 'unbroken peace.'

497–498. *men only . . . rational,* among rational creatures only men disagree.

498. *though,* 'and they do so although . . .'

499. *God proclaiming peace,* 'though God proclaims peace.'

501. *levy,* 'raise,' as we speak of levying troops.

504. *enow,* 'enough.'

506. *Stygian.* See note on I, 239.

508. *Midst,* 'in the midst.'

508. *paramount,* 'supreme lord.'

509. *Alone, i.e.,* sufficient by himself.

511. *god-like imitated state,* 'the imitation of a god-like state.'

512. *globe* probably means a dense throng, as the Latin *globus* often does. But some people think it means an actual sphere or globular mass, since the angels could easily hover in such a formation.

513. *emblazonry*, shields or armour with heraldic devices. *Cf.* I, 538 and note.

513. *horrent*, like "horrid" (63), means both 'bristling' and 'terrifying.'

514. *their session ended*, 'their assembly which had just ended.'

517. *sounding alchymy*. Alchymy (or alchemy) is the art of transmuting metals, particularly base metals, into gold. But the word is also used of an alloy resembling gold. (In an old book on metallurgy we are told that "tin and brass make alchymy.") Here of course it means trumpets made of such metal.

518. *By harald's voice explained*. The details were given in an official proclamation following the trumpet-call.

On the form "harald" see the note on I, 752.

521 *ff*. For the meaning of the devil's various pastimes see Introduction, p. 34.

521. *Thence . . . minds*, 'their troubled minds being relieved by the proclamation.'

522. *ranged*, 'drawn up in ranks.'

526. *entertain*, 'while away.'

528–569. The description of the pastimes of the devils is very like Virgil's description of those of the spirits of the dead in Elysium (*Aeneid* VI, 642–665), and Milton may well have been thinking of this. Both the spirits in Elysium and the devils indulge in various sports, in music, and in philosophy, and both have military equipment, horses and chariots, though those of the spirits are inactive at the moment. The devils are able to add the interests of exploration.

528. *sublime*, 'aloft.'

528–530. Some hold flying races in the air, others running races on the ground. (Notice the reversal of the phrases: "on the plain" goes with "in swift race," "in the air sublime" with "upon the wing.")

530. *Olympian games.* These were the greatest national games of the Greeks, held every five years at Olympia in Elis. They included various contests—races, wrestling, boxing, riding, chariot races, etc.—and ended with a general festival and feasts in honour of the victors. Besides the competitors, envoys from all the Greek states and colonies attended, and the sanctity of the games was so great that during the time of the celebration there was a general truce throughout the Greek world.

530. *Pythian fields* (= games). These were similar to the Olympian games, but included musical and artistic competitions. They were held at Delphi.

531. *curb their fiery steeds. I.e.*, horse-races.

531. *shun the goal* refers not to what we mean by a goal, but to the arrangements in a Roman chariot race. In this there was a low wall down the middle of the course, with conical pillars ("goals") at each end; the competitors had to go round the course seven times, and it was naturally extremely difficult to guide the excited horses round the posts without wrecking the chariot.

532. *fronted*, 'drawn up facing one another.'

532. *brigads*. On this form of the word see note on I, 675. The devils hold a military display.

533–538. This is generally explained as a description of the Aurora Borealis, but such portents are supposed to have been seen before various dire events, which they were regarded as foretelling ("to warn proud cities"). So, for instance, before Caesar's death, as related by Calpurnia in Shakespeare, *Julius Caesar* II, ii, 19–20:

Fierce fiery warriors fight upon the clouds,
In ranks and squadrons and right form of war.

and before the fall of Jerusalem similar portents were said to have been seen.

535. *van:* the first line, or vanguard.

536. *Prick,* 'ride' (spur on a horse).

536. *couch.* To 'couch' a spear means to lower it and fix it against a 'rest' or socket in the rider's armour, ready for the attack.

538. *welkin,* 'sky.'

539. *Typhoean.* On Typhoeus or Typhon see note on I, 199. Typhoean rage = rage like that of Typhoeus.

539. *fell,* 'fierce.' Agreeing with "others."

542. *Alcides:* Heracles (Hercules), grandson of Alcaeus. The story goes that Heracles had been away for a long time, on an expedition against the King of Oechalia. On his way back he wished to sacrifice to Zeus in thankfulness for his victory. He therefore sent his friend Lichas to ask his wife Deianira to send him a suitable robe. Deianira, suspecting Heracles of unfaithfulness, sent him one dipped in what she believed to be a love-potion, but what was really the blood of the centaur Nessus, whom Heracles had killed with a poisoned arrow and which was therefore itself poisonous. When Lichas brought it and Heracles put it on, it burned him, causing great agony which drove him mad. He tore up trees by the roots, and rocks, and finally seized Lichas and threw him into the sea. In the end he returned home, and unable to endure the suffering, from which there was no escape as the robe stuck to his flesh, he climbed Mount Oeta, built a funeral pyre for himself, and having caused it to be set alight, was carried up to heaven in a cloud and became immortal.

Milton follows a version which makes Mount Oeta the scene of the death of Lichas.

542. *from*, sc. 'coming.'

544. *Thessalian*, because Mount Oeta is in Thessaly.

546. *Euboic sea:* the sea between the east coast of Greece and the island of Euboea.

546. *more mild*, as contrasted with "others more fell" (539).

547. *Retreated*, 'having retired.'

551. *enthrall*, 'enslave.'

551. *virtue* probably means 'courage' or 'nobility' as generally at this period, not virtue in our sense of the word.

552. *partial*, 'biased'—in favour of themselves, as is evident from the previous lines.

553. *What could it less? I.e.*, 'What less could it do? What less was to be expected of it?'

554. *Suspended*, 'held in suspense,' with rapt attention.

554. *took*, 'captivated,' 'enchanted,' a very frequent meaning of the word in this period. *Cf. Nativity Ode*, 98, "As all their souls in blissful rapture took," and Shakespeare, *Winter's Tale* IV, iv, 119–120, "take/The winds of March with beauty."

558. *elevate* (= elevated) probably agrees with "others" (557).

559–560. These topics, especially that of free will and predestination, were often and earnestly discussed by theologians of Milton's time; he himself discusses them later through the words of God in III, 96 *ff*, and X, 34 *ff*.

Note the careful rhetoric, suggesting the involved arguments of the devils, going round in circles as it were—the words in line 560 repeating those of 559 in inverse order and with the addition of appropriate adjectives.

562–565. These topics are those in which the Greek and Roman philosophers were particularly interested. They sought especially the *summum bonum* or supreme good, which the Epicureans found in pleasure, the Stoics in freedom from all passion.

564. *Passion*, 'feeling.'

564. *apathy*, the opposite of "passion"—insensibility to all feeling, whether of pleasure or of pain; the Stoic ideal.

568. *obdured*, 'hardened,' the Latin meaning. The accent is on the first syllable.

569. *triple steel*, 'threefold armour'—a phrase from Horace.

570. *gross*, 'large.' For Milton's problems in introducing the classical rivers of Hades see Introduction, p. 13.

571. *discover*, 'explore.'

571. *wide*, 'far and wide.'

572. *clime*, 'place.' *Cf.* I, 242.

573. *bend . . . march*, 'fly off in four directions'—along the banks of the four rivers.

575–581. The four rivers in classical mythology marked the boundaries of Hades (Hell). Their Greek names correspond in meaning to the descriptive phrases Milton gives—hate, sorrow, lamentation, and flame.

581. *torrent* may refer to the stream, which was of fire instead of water, or it may have the Latin meaning of 'burning.'

581. *inflame*, 'are on fire.'

583. *Lethe:* a river which flowed through Hades. The souls of the dead drank from it and forthwith forgot all their past life.

584. *watery labyrinth:* streams forming a maze or network.

587–603. The belief that the torments of Hell included freezing as well as burning was general in the Middle Ages, and probably goes back to Jewish tradition. Dante gives a famous description of the torments of the damned by cold in the ninth circle of Hell (*Inferno*, xxxii), and Shakespeare alludes to the belief in *Measure for Measure* III, i, 119 *ff.*

588. *beat*, 'beaten.'

590. *gathers heap*, 'heaps up.'

590. *ruin . . . pile*, 'looks like the ruins of some ancient building.'

591. *all else deep snow and ice*. Where the ground is firm the hail is heaped up high, but everywhere else there is deep snow and ice.

592. *Serbonian bog:* Lake Serbonis, near Damiata (now Damietta) on the eastern estuary of the Nile. It was a quicksand rather than a lake, although there was a small lake in the centre. It is recorded that a considerable part of a Persian army marching on Egypt was lost there, but "armies whole" is an exaggeration based on an ancient historian.

592. *Mount Casius:* a range of sandstone hills to the south of Lake Serbonis.

594–595. A passage from the Apocryphal book of Ecclesiasticus (xliii, 20–21) has been quoted as a parallel to this idea: "[the cold north wind] burneth the wilderness, and consumeth the grass as fire."

In actual fact any one who has experienced frost-bite knows that it feels like burning.

594. *parching*, 'drying,' not necessarily through heat. One can be 'parched with thirst' even in the Arctic.

595. *frore*. An old form of 'frozen.' Country folk in East Anglia still say they are 'frorn' with cold.

596. *harpy-footed*. The Harpies, in classical mythology, were monsters in the form of great birds, with wings and hooked claws, but with the faces of maidens.

596. *Furies:* goddesses who pursued those guilty of such crimes as murder.

596. *haled*, 'dragged.' A 'haling way' is a path alongside a canal for the horses which dragged barges along.

597. *revolutions*, 'recurring periods of time.'

600. *starve*, 'freeze,' as still in some dialects in the intransitive sense though here it is transitive.

601. *soft ethereal warmth*. Being angels and therefore made of "empyreal" (*i.e.*, fiery) substance, their natural warmth would make them suffer all the more from cold.

603. *Periods of time*: the "revolutions" of line 597.

604. *ferry*, used intransitively here.

604. *Lethean sound*: the river of Lethe, which they had crossed to reach the frozen land (587).

604. *sound*, 'strait'; *cf.* "sounds and seas" (*Comus*, 115). Here it means 'river.'

606-609. Milton here seems to let pity for the tormented devils dominate him and us. The phrases "wish and struggle," "one small drop," "all in one moment," and "so near the brink" make one feel how little they needed, and how nearly they attained it, only to lose it after all, and thereby "augment their sorrow."

They are prevented by three things—Fate, Medusa, and the retreat of the water.

611. *Medusa* was one of the three monstrous sisters called Gorgons. Her face was very beautiful, but she had snakes instead of hair. Whoever looked at her was turned into stone. Perseus was able to kill her through looking at her reflection in a mirror to avoid seeing her actual face. The head of Medusa formed the centre of Athene's (Minerva's) shield.

613. *wight*, 'person.'

614. *Tantalus* was punished by Zeus for a crime (of which various accounts are given) by being made to stand in a lake up to his neck; he endured terrible thirst; but whenever he tried to drink from the lake the water receded beyond his reach. (The lake was however not the same as the river Lethe.) He was also tormented by hunger which he tried to satisfy with the fruit of trees which hung over his head; but these too constantly eluded him. We get the word 'tantalize' from this story, though we may not always realize the fact.

617. *Viewed first,* 'saw for the first time.'

617. *lot, i.e.,* place allotted to them, their portion.

617–618. *found/No rest.* Milton may have had in mind the words of Christ, "When the unclean spirit is gone out of a man, he walketh through dry places, seeking rest, and findeth none." (St Matthew xii, 43, and St Luke xi, 24.)

619. *dolorous,* 'full of grief.'

620. *alp* originally means any high mountain, as here.

621. All these monosyllables, so difficult to pronounce, suggest the dreariness of the landscape and the difficulty of the journey.

625. *prodigious,* 'portentous,' 'monstrous.'

627. *fables:* the legends of classical mythology. See note on I, 197.

628. *Gorgon.* See note on Medusa (611).

628. *Hydras.* The Hydra was a huge water-snake which had nine heads; when one of these was cut off, two grew in its place. The monster was killed by Hercules.

628. *Chimaeras.* The Chimaera was a creature partly lion, partly goat, and partly serpent, which breathed out fire. It was finally killed by Bellerophon.

Virgil speaks of the Hydra, the Chimaera, and the Gorgon among other monsters which guard the entrance to Hell. (*Aeneid* VI, 287–289.)

629. *the Adversary of God and Man,* because Satan's enterprise is now directed against Man, as well as against God as before.

631. *Puts on swift wings* is of course not intended literally, since Satan already had wings, but means 'flies swiftly.' *Cf.* 700, "to thy speed add wings."

632. *Explores.* Satan had set forth on an exploring expedition "in search of this new world" (403 *ff.*). The expression "explores his flight" combines the idea of 'explores his way' with that of 'pursues his flight.'

633. *scours*, 'passes swiftly over.'

634. *shaves*, 'skims,' like a swallow. This line seems to be directly imitated from Virgil's description of the flight of a dove. "She shaves the liquid way and moves not her swift wings." (*Aeneid* V, 217.)

635. *the fiery concave:* the roof of Hell, *cf.* note on 434.

637. *Hangs in the clouds* as ships often seem to do, when the line of the horizon melts into the sky.

637. *equinoctial winds*, probably the winds which blow on the equator (the 'equinoctial line'), but possibly those which blow at the time of the equinoxes, called the 'trade winds.'

638. *Close, i.e.,* close together, so that they seem to be a single object.

638. *Bengala:* Bengal.

639. *Ternate and Tidore:* two of the Moluccas or Spice Islands in the Malay Straits.

640. *they:* the ships.

640. *trading flood:* the sea which served traders; "trading" in the same sense as in 'trade winds.'

641. *Ethiopian, sc.* sea. Milton clearly means the sea along the east coast of Africa, part of what is now called the Indian Ocean. The name was more often applied to the sea on the west of Africa, or even to the whole ocean south of the equator.

641. *the Cape, sc.* of Good Hope.

642. *stemming*, 'keeping their course.' The stem of a vessel is the timber forming the prow, so "stemming" gives the picture of the ship's prow cutting through the sea.

642. *the pole* must be the South Pole, since the ships are steering southwards to round the Cape of Good Hope.

642. *so seemed* brings the comparison to an end, referring back to "As when . . ." (636). The point of the comparison is the resemblance between Satan as he flew

aloft to a ship seen far away at sea, but Milton is led on to introduce this exciting and romantic description of the voyage of the East Indiamen from the Malay archipelago down the east coast of Africa and round the Cape of Good Hope (there being no short cut through the Suez Canal) to bring their valuable cargoes of spice to Europe. The trade was a new one, so there are the interests both of actuality and of romance.

647. *impaled*, surrounded as with a paling or fence.

649 *ff.* For a comment on the allegorical figures of Sin and Death see Introduction, p. 35.

649. *formidable* had a much stronger meaning in Milton's day than it has now—'terrifying.'

650. *The one*. This is Sin, though we do not know this until she herself tells us in line 760. Milton's picture of Sin closely resembles that of Error in Spenser's *Faerie Queene* (I, i, 13–15), which Milton certainly knew. One of Spenser's followers, Phineas Fletcher (*The Purple Island*, xii, 27, 28) has a very similar description of Sin (whom he calls by a Greek name, Hamartia). Both Spenser and Fletcher give pictures of a creature half woman, half serpent, with a long tail ending in a sting, and Spenser's "Error" is surrounded by a brood of her young which creep inside her when alarmed. However, the hell-hounds which surround Sin seem to be suggested rather by the barking dogs which surround Scylla (see note on 660). In another poem (*The Apollyonists*, i, 10) Fletcher says, "The Porter to the infernal gate is Sin," and goes on to give a description of Sin which is very much like Milton's description of Death (666–673).

Allegories such as this of Sin and Death are common in the Middle Ages. The basis of this one may be found in the Epistle of St James (i, 15), "Then when lust hath conceived, it bringeth forth sin: and sin, when it is finished, bringeth forth death." Milton puts Satan in the place of lust, and adds the further complication of the marriage of Sin and Death.

652. *Voluminous* probably means 'twisting.'

653. *mortal*, 'causing death,' *cf.* 'mortal wound.'

653. *sting*, perhaps suggested by I Corinthians, xv, 56, "The sting of death is sin."

653. *round*, a 'coil' of her snaky tail.

654. *cry*, 'pack.'

655. *Cerberean*, like those of Cerberus, the three-headed dog which guarded the classical Hell. (Scan 'Cerbérean.')

655. *rung/A hideous peal*, as if they were like a sort of horrible church bells.

656. *list* (= listed) 'wished.'

659. *Far less abhorred*, '[hounds] far less detestable.'

660. *vexed*, 'troubled.' *Cf.* I, 306, "Hath vexed the Red Sea coast."

660. *Scylla* was a beautiful maiden beloved by the sea-god Glaucus who begged the help of the enchantress Circe to win her love. Circe, however, being jealous of her, put magic herbs into the sea where Scylla was accustomed to bathe, and so transformed her into a monstrous creature, with the head and body of a woman but with the tail of a fish, and surrounded by barking dogs. Scylla was supposed to live on a rock on the Italian side of the Straits of Messina, where the sea was very rough and dangerous; the constant roar of the waves is supposed to have given rise to the myth of the barking dogs.

661. *Calabria:* the 'toe' of Italy.

661. *hoarse* from the noise of the waves.

661. *Trinacria:* Sicily (the 'three-cornered' island).

662. *nor uglier, sc.* 'hounds,' as in 659 above.

662. *night-hag:* probably Hecate, the goddess of magic and queen of the witches. In Shakespeare's *Macbeth* (IV, i) Hecate appears to the witches at their incantation.

662. *called*, invoked or summoned.

664. *riding through the air* like a witch on a broomstick.

664. *infant blood*. Witches were believed to kill children.

665. *Lapland* was regarded as the stronghold of witches and sorcerers.

665. *labouring*, 'going into eclipse.' The word was often used of the sun and moon in Latin, in this sense.

666. *at their charms*. The belief that the moon can be made to come down to the earth, to be eclipsed, or to behave in any other desired manner by the use of charms has been common in all ages and places.

This passage (662–666) sounds fantastic to us, but of course in Milton's time the belief in witchcraft persisted.

666-673. Milton, unlike lesser writers, does not attempt to describe the indescribable, but by his very vagueness gives the feeling of horror which definite details would have destroyed.

670. *each seemed either*. I.e., if it were substance, it seemed like shadow, or if it were shadow, it seemed like substance.

671. *Furies*. See note on 596.

672. *what seemed his head*. The suggestive indefiniteness of "seemed" and "likeness" is most striking.

677. *admired*, 'wondered.' See note on I, 690.

678-679. *God . . . shunned*, 'he neither respected nor feared anything except God and his Son.' Quibblers object that "God and his Son" are included among "created things," but the meaning is perfectly clear.

681. *execrable*, 'accursed.'

683. *miscreated*, 'misshapen,' 'hideous.'

686. *taste*, 'realize by experience.' *Cf.* Psalm 34, 8, "O taste and see that the Lord is good."

692. *the third part*. See note on I, 633.

693. *Conjured*, 'banded together by an oath,' the meaning of the Latin *conjurare*. Accent 'conjúred.'

695. *waste*, 'spend.'

697. *Hell-doomed*. Death's reply to Satan's taunt "Hell-born" (687).

701. *a whip of scorpions*. *Cf.* Rehoboam's words in I Kings xii, 11 and 14, "my father hath chastised you with whips, but I will chastise you with scorpions." The scorpions are of course metaphorical.

702. *Thy lingering*, 'thee if thou lingerest.'

702. *or with*, 'or (lest) with. . . .'

706. *deform* = 'deformed,' *i.e.*, 'ugly'—the meaning of the Latin word *deformis*. So in the *Nativity Ode*, 43-44, Nature is

> Confounded, that her Maker's eyes
> Should look so near upon her foul deformities.

707. *Incensed*, 'aflame,' or 'burning.' Satan was on fire both literally, like a comet, and metaphorically, with indignation.

709. *Ophiouchus*: 'the serpent-bearer,' a large constellation in the northern hemisphere which was supposed to resemble a man holding a serpent.

710. *horrid*, 'shaggy.'

710. *hair*. The word 'comet' literally means 'hairy' [star].

711. *Shakes* gives a vivid picture of the comet scattering destruction. Comets, like eclipses (see note on I, 597) were believed to portend disaster.

   The comparison of Satan to these vast astronomical objects gives the impression of his magnitude and splendour. A similar comparison was made by Virgil, who likens Aeneas in his dazzling armour to a comet blazing threateningly. (*Aeneid* X, 270-273.)

711. *at the head*, *sc.* 'of his opponent.'

712. *fatal*, 'death-dealing.'

714. *two black clouds*. The difficulty of pronouncing these words illustrates "come rattling on" (715).

715. *Heaven's artillery:* thunder and lightning, an expression used by Shakespeare and other Elizabethan poets.

715. *fraught,* 'laden.'

716. *the Caspian* was proverbially stormy.

717. *a space,* 'for a little while.'

717. *blow* in a double sense—the winds blow, as a trumpet blows the signal.

721. *but once more:* when they were to encounter their great foe, Christ, and be defeated by him.

723. *Had been,* 'would have been.'

724. *the snaky sorceress:* Sin (see 650–653).

725. *fatal* here means 'fateful.'

727. *intends,* 'purposes.'

730. *and knowst,* 'although thou knowest.'

731. *and laughs,* as Belial said (191), "All these our motions vain sees and derides."

732. *ordained as drudge,* as Beelzebub had said of the devils (I, 149).

735. *the hellish pest:* Death.

736. *these, sc.* 'words.'

739. *spares to,* 'refrains from.'

749. *the assembly* of Satan and his allies, at which they determined to rebel. (V, 767 *ff.*)

757. *a goddess . . . sprung,* as Athene sprang fully armed from the head of Zeus, according to the Greek legend: another instance of the fusion of classical and biblical elements, since the reference to the Epistle of St James (see note on 650) is also in Milton's mind.

761. *Portentous,* 'like a portent,' *i.e.,* foreboding evil.

764. *Thyself . . . viewing,* 'seeing a perfect copy of thyself in me.'

768. *fields,* 'battles'; *cf.* I, 105.

769. *what could else,* 'what else was possible?'

770 *ff. Cf.* I, 44 *ff.*

771. *the Empyrean:* Heaven. See note on I, 117.

771-772. *Down they fell . . . down.* Most effective repetition.

772. *pitch*, 'height,' *cf.* 'the pitch of one's voice,' 'such a pitch of insolence,' 'a high-pitched roof.'

783. *that*, 'so that.'

784. *my nether shape*, 'the lower part of my body.'

785. *inbred*, 'nurtured within me.'

788. *Hell trembled.* So in IX, 1000, Earth trembles when Adam eats the forbidden fruit.

789. *Death*, the echo of Sin's cry. Milton may have got the idea of this poetic device from Virgil, *Georgics* IV, 525-527, where the banks of the river echo "Eurydice" to Orpheus' cry.

801. *conscious* here has the meaning 'present to consciousness,' or 'making conscious,' rather like "oblivious" in I, 266 (see note there). Sin means that even when the hell-hounds have for the time being ceased to gnaw her, she is still conscious of the pain and knows that the hell-hounds will return.

802. *that*, 'so that,' as in 783.

803. *in opposition*, 'opposite,' *i.e.*, on the other side of the gate of Hell (see 649).

807. *His end with mine involved.* As death came into the world with sin, so it must end when sin ends.

809. *Fate.* Sin, like Satan (I, 116), believes Fate to be the supreme power.

813. *tempered heavenly.* Satan's shield was described as "ethereal temper" in I, 285 (see note).

813. *mortal dint*, 'deadly blow.'

814. *Save he.* We would now say 'save him,' but the nominative was usual in Milton's time. *Cf.* Shakespeare, *Julius Caesar* V, v, 69, "All the conspirators save only he."

815. *lore*, 'lesson.' Satan has learnt through Sin's revelation to speak more gently and cautiously. There is a great difference between his tone in 744-745 and 817-818.

825. *pretences*, 'claims.' *Cf.* the use of 'Pretender' = 'claimant to the throne.'

826–829. Satan repeats the undertaking he gave to the devils in 463–466.

827. *uncouth.* See note on 407.

827. *sole*, 'alone.'

829. *unfounded*, 'bottomless.'

830. *a place foretold.* Satan had already mentioned this prophecy to the devils (I, 650–654) and Beelzebub had also spoken of it (II, 345–353).

830. *search, sc.* 'for.'

830–831. *a place foretold/Should be*, 'A place which it was foretold would come into existence.'

831–832. *by concurring . . ./Created*, 'which must by now have been created, to judge by various signs leading to the same conclusion.'

832. *a place of bliss* contrasted with "this dark and dismal house of pain" (823).

833. *purlieus*, 'borders.'

835. *our vacant room*, 'the place we once occupied, now empty.'

835. *more removed*, 'further off.'

836. *surcharged*, 'overburdened,' 'overcrowded.'

837. *broils*, 'disturbances,' 'turmoils.'

837–838. *Be this . . . now designed*, 'Whether this or something even more secret is planned.'

840–844. Satan amply fulfils his promise to Sin and Death, when he has succeeded in his quest and Adam and Eve have fallen to his temptation. In X, 397–409 he summons Sin and Death to rule the earth, including man:

> You two this way, among these numerous orbs
> All yours, right down to Paradise descend:
> There dwell and reign in bliss, thence on the Earth
> Dominion exercise and in the air.
> Chiefly on Man, sole lord of all declared;
> Him first make sure you thrall and lastly kill.

847. *famine,* 'ravenous hunger.'

847. *maw,* 'stomach,' properly applied to animals. Eve uses the same words when she speaks of Death's "ravenous maw" (X, 991).

849. *bespake,* 'addressed.'

850. *by due,* 'by right,' or 'as my due.'

855. *Fearless to be,* 'not afraid of being '

856. *his commands above,* 'the commands of him above.'

858. *Tartarus.* See note on 69.

860. *Inhabitant of Heaven* belongs with "me" (857).

868. *The gods who live at ease.* A phrase from Homer.

869. *at thy right hand.* Sin as Satan's daughter impiously claims to sit at his right hand, like the Son at the right hand of the Father.

869. *voluptuous,* 'in pleasure.'

873. *bestial train:* the serpent-like part of her body (651–653).

874. *portcullis:* a grating used to reinforce the actual gate of a castle. It was raised or lowered along grooves at the side.

875. *Stygian.* See note on I, 239.

877. *intricate:* the accent is on the second syllable.

880. Note the jolting rhythm reinforcing the sense.

883. *Erebus:* the lowest part of Hell.

883–884. Only God, after the Last Judgement, will shut the gates of Hell.

889. *redounding,* 'billowing.'

890. Milton now describes Chaos, the confused heap of matter out of which God creates things (see Introduction, p. 29).

891. *secrets,* 'hidden places' or 'recesses'; *cf.* 972.

894–895. Chaos is not only a heap of matter, but, according to classical mythology, a personified figure with whom Night, another such figure, is associated. Chaos is a realm of sheer disorder, and darkness or Night is appropriate to it. Light accompanies creation. Night and Chaos are ancestors of nature because out of the disorderly elements they inhabit the natural world was engendered.

898. These "champions" are the four elements, out of whose different mixture worldly phenomena were thought to arise.

900. *embryon*, 'embryonic.'

901. *Of each his faction*, 'each of his own faction.'

903. *unnumbered*, innumerable.

904. *Barca:* a desert district between Egypt and Tunis, roughly Libya.

904. *Cyrene:* an ancient Greek city on the coast of the district, opposite Crete.

905. *Levied* qualifies "sands" and means simultaneously 'uplifted' and 'enrolled' in the military sense. Before "poise" understand 'to.' The sands are enrolled to take sides with, and to give weight to, the fighting winds, which, unweighted by the sand, would be too light for the battle.

906. *To whom*, 'to whichever champion.' "These" refers to the atoms.

909–910. *arbiter*, 'judge.' (See note on I, 785.) The addition of Chance to Chaos as judge serves to increase the confusion.

911. *and perhaps her grave.* In Book XII, 546 Milton says that at the last day the Son will "dissolve/Satan with his perverted world" but he does not say whether the world will be annihilated or dissolved into its original chaotic elements. Here he implies that the second of these methods of dissolution is probable.

912. *sea*, 'water': *shore*, 'earth.' The four elements again.

916. The possibility of multiple worlds was much discussed in Milton's day.

917–918. *Into . . . looked*, i.e., 'standing . . . looked into';

cf. V, 368, "What the garden choicest bears/To sit and taste" (= sitting, to taste).

919. *frith*, 'straits.'

920. *pealed*, 'dinned.'

921. *ruinous*, 'crashing.'

922. *Bellona:* the goddess of war.

923. *engines* may include cannon as well as more old-fashioned siege-instruments such as battering-rams. See note on I, 750.

924-927. *this frame / Of heaven*, 'this celestial structure.' Probably "heaven" here refers not to God's dwelling but to the skies above the earth. The 'structure' then will be the universe.

926. *axle* is a strange word here because it implies motion in the thing that surrounds it. But it also has the quality of fixity, and Milton is thinking of this quality when he goes on to talk of the "stedfast earth."

927. *sail-broad*, 'spreading like sails.' Sailing and flying are comparable activities. This idea appears in the comparison of Satan flying to the sailing ships (631 *ff.*).

927. *vans*, 'wings.'

930. *cloudy chair*, 'chair made of clouds.'

933. *pennons*, 'pinions.'

934. *fadom*, Milton's form of 'fathom.'

937. *Instinct with*, 'impregnated with.'

938. *that fury stayed*, 'that furious rebound having been halted.'

939. *Quenched*, 'brought to a standstill.'

939. *Syrtis:* a quicksand on the North African coast; here meaning any kind of quicksand.

940. *foundered*, 'sunk.'

941. *crude consistence*, 'imperfect mixture of water and earth.'

942. *behoves*, 'it behoves him (he needs)' *sc.* 'to use.'

943. *Gryphon.* In *Alice in Wonderland* the King, the Queen, and Alice "came upon a Gryphon, lying fast asleep in

the sun," and the author adds, "If you don't know what
a gryphon is, look at the picture." And Tenniel has
drawn his gryphon (or griffin) quite correctly with the
upper half like an eagle and the lower half like a lion.
Pictures of gryphons occur in the medieval books of
beasts.

943–947. According to classical legend the Arimaspians
were a one-eyed race living in what is now southern
Russia. They warred with the Gryphons, who had
stores of gold they had extracted from the earth. The
dragon, or griffin, or snake with its hoard of gold is
common in Germanic as well as in classical mythology.
In fighting the Arimaspians Milton pictures the Gryphons moving like ostriches, half running and half flying.

Milton knew the classical legends and he had probably seen a picture of a Gryphon in a medieval bestiary.
He uses this queer comparison to make queerer and
more grotesque Satan's plight as he battles his way
through Chaos.

948–950. Satan's struggle through Chaos is vividly suggested by these three strange and powerful lines made
up entirely of monosyllables. Milton used the same
method to describe the journey of the devils in 621.

951. *universal hubbub.* It is fitting that Chaos and Night
with their attendants should have their headquarters
or palace in the place where the uproar is at its
height. Satan knows this and therefore seeks the
noisiest place.

954. *plies.* Milton probably intends the technical nautical
sense of 'beats up against the wind.'

959. *straight,* 'immediately.'

960. *pavilion,* 'tent.'

961. *wasteful,* 'desolate.'

962. *sable-vested,* 'robed in black.'

964. *Orcus and Ades*, the Latin and Greek names respectively for both Hell and Hell's ruler. Here they are vague personifications of a realm of disorder. ("Ades" is usually spelt 'Hades.')

964–965. *dreaded name of Demogorgon* is a Latinism meaning 'Demogorgon himself.' Demogorgon was a mysterious infernal power mentioned in late Latin literature and popularized in the Renaissance. Spenser (*Faerie Queene* IV, ii, 47) had already associated Demogorgon and Chaos.

965–967. Several Renaissance poets, describing the nether regions, introduced personified qualities like these. The habit is derived from Virgil's description of Orcus in *Aeneid* VI, 273 *ff.*

972. *secrets*. See note on 891.

973. *Wandering, sc.* 'through.'

976. *What readiest path . . . Heaven*, 'the shortest way to the point at which the realm of Chaos borders on Heaven.'

977. *Confine with*, 'border on.'

978. *From your dominion won*. As Chaos himself complains (1000–1006) his dominion had been diminished by the creation first of Hell and then of the universe. He wishes to divert from himself to God any anger that Chaos may feel on account of his intrusion; and he succeeds.

980. *travel this profound*, 'traverse this gulf.'

981. *Directed*, 'if my course is directed.'

982. *behoof*, 'benefit.'

982. *that region lost:* the newly created universe.

985. *Which is my present journey*. Understand the words 'the object of' after "is."

988. *Anarch*. Milton coined this word and meant by it the upholder or prince of anarchy, Chaos.

989. *incomposed*, 'disturbed.'

992. *Made head against*, 'rose in insurrection against.'

995. *ruin*, 'downfall'; *cf.* I, 46 and note.

996. *Confusion worse confounded* has become a familiar quotation used in a vague sense, but the real meaning is that Chaos itself has become more chaotic.

999. *if all I can,* 'in hope that my best endeavours.'

1000. *so, i.e.,* by residing there.

1001. *intestine broils:* the wars of the elements. These resemble civil wars, and occupy Chaos to the detriment of his defence against the encroachments of God.

1002–1006. See Introduction, p. 29.

1004. *heaven:* the sky of the universe; see note on 924–927.

1005. *a golden chain.* See note on 1051.

1006. *Heaven.* This time God's Heaven is meant.

1013. *pyramid of fire.* Milton may wish us to think of Satan rising like a rocket.

1017–1018. The Argo in Greek mythology was the first ocean-going ship. On it Jason and his men sailed from Greece through the Bosphorus to fetch the Golden Fleece from near the eastern end of the Black Sea. Their passage had to be between two floating rocks that kept clashing together. By a subtle piece of timing the Argo got safely through. The comparison is especially apt because, as the Argo was the first ship to brave the ocean, so Satan was the first living creature to cross Chaos of his own free will.

1019–1020. This second comparison is also to a sea-voyage: to that between Italy and Sicily. Here was a narrow passage between rocks, and in it were dangerous whirlpools. One rock was Scylla, on which a monster of that name lived (see note on 660) and the other was Charybdis. Ulysses steers to the "larboard," or left, near Scylla, thus avoiding Charybdis. He got through but lost two of his companions snatched off the boat by the monster.

1021–1022. We have seen how in lines 621 and 948–950 Milton suggested the difficulty of the journey by using a succession of monosyllables. Here he uses a different method—first, the scansion of the lines is itself difficult; secondly, Milton repeats the phrases; and thirdly, he reverses their order. He has used a similar method in the description of the hugeness of Leviathan (I, 202).

1024. *amain*, 'without delay.'

1024–1030. Milton describes the building of this bridge or causeway in X, 293 *ff*. For its exact nature see Introduction, p. 30.

1029. *utmost orb:* the outer shell enclosing the world. See Introduction, p. 29.

1030. *frail*, 'fallible,' referring to the possibility of the Fall and of the world's consequent corruption.

1030. *perverse*, 'perverted.'

1033. The belief in certain angels specially commissioned to protect mankind was widely current in Milton's day.

1034. *sacred*, because "light" symbolizes God and Heaven. The third book, dealing at first with Heaven, begins with an invocation to light; and the rest of the second book not only concludes Satan's journey from Hell to the region of light but serves to introduce the third book.

1034. *influence*, 'flowing in,' the literal meaning.

1037–1038. 'Here the farthest frontier of nature (creation or the universe) begins.'

1038. *fardest*. See note on I, 247.

1038. *to retire*, sc. 'begins.'

1039. *As from her outmost works*. The metaphor is of a military frontier of a great empire. Milton may even have been thinking of the frontier of civilized Rome with the barbarians beyond. Nature here has her outposts, from which hostile Chaos is beaten back.

1041. *That*, 'so that.'

1042. *Wafts*, 'voyages'—an intransitive use of the verb.

1043. *holds*, 'makes his way towards.'

1046. *Weighs,* 'keeps even,' like a bird hovering.

1048. *circuit:* dimension generally, without any notion of rotundity.

1048. *undetermined square or round.* "Undetermined" agrees with "Heaven" and one has to understand 'whether it is' after it.

1049-1050. There is clearly some reference here to the jewels mentioned in the description of Heaven in Revelation xxi, 18-21.

1051. For the physical arrangement of the universe as here described, see Introduction, p. 29.

The origin of the idea of the golden chain is to be found in Homer (*Iliad* VIII, 18 *ff.*) where Zeus claims that he could pull up to himself the earth and sky by a golden chain, to prove his superior power to the other gods. The idea was used by many later writers, who attached various allegorical meanings to it. In Milton's day this symbolism was current, the chain being the bond between the divine and the human.

1052-1053. Milton is thinking not of the actual size of moon and stars but of their aspect to the naked eye. The whole universe compared with Heaven looked as tiny as the tiniest-looking star alongside the full moon.

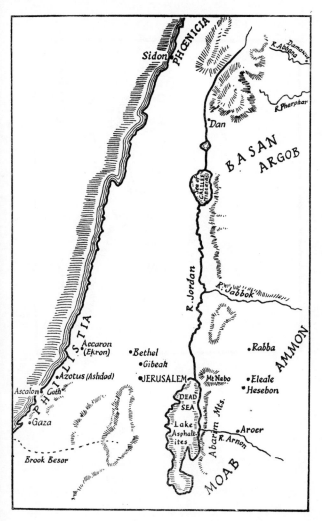

PALESTINE

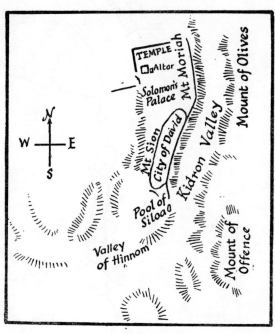

JERUSALEM